YOUR
HEALTH
—— AND ——
HEALING

Living Life God's Way

GWENDOLYN GATTISON

Your Health & Healing
Living Life God's Way

Gwendolyn Gattison
gwen1953@live.com

ISBN: 978-1-943342-63-1

Printed in the USA.
All rights reserved

Published by: Destined To Publish | Flossmoor, Illinois
www.DestinedToPublish.com

To

From

DEDICATION

This book is dedicated to all who need a physical and spiritual touch from the Lord. To those who feel they are not connected to God for whatever reason. To those who have been through a lot and need to be reassured that God loves them.

It is dedicated to the one who is struggling with an addiction, the person who thinks they need a divorce, the one who is contemplating something drastic, the person who feels the weight of the world is upon their shoulders, the little girl or little boy who is now all grown up but continues to labor with that childhood traumatic experiences.

I dedicate this book to my sister, who has read healing scriptures daily for the past twenty years or more. She has been persistent and steadfast in her faith to build an atmosphere conducive for healing and thriving.

and

To my amazing family, who is always supportive!

ACKNOWLEDGMENT

I want to thank my Lord and Savior, Jesus Christ, for his guidance and leadership in my life. I thank Him for opening the eyes of my understanding to see what my true calling is in life. The gift He has placed inside of me is to help individuals reach their true identity in Christ and to help them know that they are a child of God and he loves them dearly.

He has placed so many wonderful people in my life who needed assistance. I first realized this calling when I worked for a Home Health Agency that my nephew owned and operated. Getting the clients supplies, governmental assistance, medications, and sometimes a disability check was such a much needed and rewarding effort.

God has a way of showing up in our lives with unexpected blessings through unexpected assignments. He is an on-time God that never sleeps nor slumbers. The Book of Joshua tells us that when we don't let the Word of God depart from our mouths, we will be successful. Godly success can be good for our health and our well-being.

The Book of Psalms tells us to keep the Word of God in our hearts, so that we will not sin against the Lord. Keeping a pure heart will surely help us maintain a healthy body and environment.

A big thank you to my husband of fifty years for always supporting my endeavors. I would like to acknowledge Sophia Ruffin Ministries and the Ready Writers Connection Team for their support and guidance in this project.

CONTENT

God is Faithful 1

God is Everything 2

A Holy God 3

The Keeper 4

Overflow 5

Good Success 6

The Right Crowd 7

Worthy God 8

Understanding Heart 9

Praying Through 10

Operate in Humility 11

Telling No One 12

Obedience is Crucial 13

My Protector 14

Meditation of Heart 15

Stand 16

Strength 17

Trouble Don't Last 18

Worship is a Lifestyle 19

Your Desire 20

The God Life 21

Patience and Prayer 22

Talking the Right Stuff 23

Clean Heart 24

Everyday Prayer 25

The Sanctuary 26

The Secret Place 27

Long Life 28

Bless the Lord 29

The Sent Word 30

The Blessed Life 31

God's Best 32

The Hidden Word...33

The Evil Path 34

The Word is a Lamp 35

My Steps..36

Deliver Me 37

Look to the Hills 38

The Hand of the Lord...39

Search Me 40

Broken in Heart 41

Acknowledge Him..42

The Principal Thing 43

Incline Thine Ear 44

A Diligent Heart 45

Established Thoughts 46

Pleasant Ways...47

Haughty Spirit...48

Speak Life 49

Where is Your Vision 50

Beauty Does Not Last...51

The Whole Duty 52

Every Work 53

The Good Land 54

Perfect Peace 55

Stand 56

Wings of Eagles 57

Wounded 58

No Weapon 59

Higher Ground 60

My Covenant 61

I Knew Thee 62

Obey My Voice 63

The Plans 64

Restoration 65

God of All Flesh 66

Call Unto Me 67

Hope and Wait 68

A New Heart 69

My Stronghold 70

Make it Plain 71

Consider Your Ways 72

Whose Influence 73

Divine Order 74

Good Works 75

Two Masters 76

Judge Not 77

Your Destiny 78

Good Seed 79

The Mouth Speaks 80

In the Midst 81

You Shall Love..82

Watch and Pray..83

Have What You Say...84

Strong Faith...85

The Beginning..86

No Greater Love..87

What's In Your Heart...88

Free Indeed..89

Abundant Life..90

Lifted Up...91

Abide Forever...92

Ask What Ye Will...93

Believe on the Lord...94

All Things..95

Confession..96

Reasonable Service..97

Brotherly Love..98

Holiness...99

God of Peace...100

Decently and in Order..101

The Work of the Lord...102

There is Liberty...103

A New Creature...104

Praying Through..105

Grace to Endure..106

I Am Crucified..107

In the Spirit..108

Be Not Deceived..109

Be Ye Kind...110

Recognize the Enemy..111

A Good Work 112

The Mind of Christ 113

Forgetting Those Things 114

Be Careful for Nothing 115

All Things 116

All Your Needs 117

Walk Worthy 118

Do All in His Name 119

Your Speech 120

Communicating With God 121

Give Thanks 122

The Appearance of Evil 123

Material Possessions 124

The Spirit of Fear 125

Show Thyself Approve 126

A Form of Godliness 127

Role Model 128

Live By Faith 129

Diligently Seek Him 130

Different Temptations 131

Doers of the Word 132

A Sanctified Heart 133

Confess Our Sins 134

Do Good 135

Alpha and Omega 136

Whisper A Prayer 137

Daily Prayer Coverage 138

Salvation Prayer 140

GOD IS FAITHFUL

And behold, I am with thee, and will keep thee in all places whither thou goest, and will bring thee again into this land; for I will not leave thee, until I have done that which I have spoken to thee of.
Genesis 28:15 (KJV)

God is faithful to fulfill his promises. Whether we go near or far, he is with us. We are never out of his sight – and this is a good thing. No matter where we are or what we are doing in life, God is there. The scripture says if we make our bed in hell, he is there. We cannot get away from him, and he does not want to leave us. This is the kind of God that we serve. Frankly, I can't see a person not wanting to be connected to this love.

Father, thank you for being faithful to your children. For always being there for us when we are well, in need, or just by providing your goodness and mercy. Thank you for not leaving us and for being a promisekeeper. When I was out in the world doing everything I thought I was big enough to do, you still took care of me. I am so grateful for your love and your commitment to me. I am forever thankful to you. I will serve you all of my days. I love you, Father. I commit my life to you. I receive you as my Lord and Savior. Use me for your glory. Let your will be done in my life. Cover me with your blessing. Father, I am yours. Amen.

GOD IS EVERYTHING

And God said unto Moses, I AM THAT I AM: and he said, Thus shalt thou say unto the children of Israel, I AM sent me unto you.
Exodus 3:14 (KJV)

God is everything that we need. He is all-inclusive. Whatever problem, circumstance, or situation we are facing, God is the solution. He sees all, knows all, and can be everywhere simultaneously. Nothing gets past him. He is an all-seeing God. He is a deliverer. He brought the children of Israel out of the wilderness. He will deliver you from your wilderness experience. Call on him. He's waiting to hear from you.

Father, I thank you for being all that I need. Whatever situation I find myself in, you are there for me. When I need a doctor, you are a healer. When I finsd myself in a legal battle, you are my lawyer. When there is confusion in the midst, you bring peace. When I feel depressed or unhappy, you bring joy. When others reject me, you affirm me. When I can't see my way, you are a way-maker. You are my all and all. I can call you early in the morning, at noonday, or late at night, and you are always available to listen to me. Thank you for your divine instructions. You are the great I AM, and I am so thankful. Amen.

A HOLY GOD

For I am the Lord your God; ye shall therefore sanctify yourselves,
and ye shall be holy, for I am holy:
Leviticus 11:44a (KJV)

We serve a holy God, therefore we also should be holy. We separate ourselves from the world's way of doing things. We are a people disciplined and focused on God's business. If we take care of his business, he will take care of ours. We put our life in his hands and allow him to orchestrate our steps. We cannot fail with the power of God on our side. He is an ever-present help. We need him every day, and every day we should give him the honor he so deserves.

Father God, thank you for being sovereign, supreme, and Lord of my life. I look to you because all my help comes from you. You are Lord of Lords and King of Kings. I consecrate myself before you. I present my body as a living sacrifice, holy and acceptable unto you. I want to do your perfect will. I will not live as the world lives, but I will follow your teachings. There is no one like you in all the earth. I exalt you, oh God, for you are worthy of all praises. I dedicate my entire life to serving you and you alone. Clean me up, Father God, so that I may be more like you. I will seek you with my whole heart. Amen.

THE KEEPER

May the Lord bless thee, and keep thee; The Lord make his face shine upon thee, and be gracious unto thee: The Lord lift up his countenance upon thee, and give thee peace.

Numbers 6:24-26 (KJV)

The Lord is a promise keeper. His answers are 'yes' and 'Amen.' He keeps us from hurt, harm, and danger. When we want to go to the left, he whispers to go to the right. There have been plenty of times when I had a desire to go one way but was prompted by a still small voice to head in a different direction. I didn't always recognize this as God speaking to me. But as I continued to read and study his word, I became more familiar with his voice.

Thank you, heavenly Father, for taking care of me when I didn't know how to care for myself and when I thought I was too grown to need anyone. Thank you for your grace, mercy, and peace. Thank you for your divine protection over my life. Father, you have always shown me great mercy and kindness. I have not always deserved your grace, but you kept me in great peace, and for that, I am so thankful. I am grateful for your love, your commitment, your faithfulness, and your compassion. I will always look to you for help because I have realized all my help comes from you. You are great and greatly to be praised. Amen.

OVERFLOW

And all these blessings shall come on thee, and overtake thee, if thou shalt
hearken unto the voice of the Lord thy God.
Deuteronomy 28:2 (KJV)

Operating in the overflow of God's blessings can be a wonderful thing. If we trust and obey our heavenly Father, he will surely cause his blessings to overtake us. Our humanity gets in the way of our relationship with the father. We trust more in ourselves than in the Almighty God. When we think we have all the answers is when we fail. If we could only follow and obey the word of the Lord, life would be so much more attractive. As God has given us the manual (Bible) with all the instructions to live a good life, this is not a hard task.

Father, I surrender my life to you. Give me ears to hear and eyes to see what thus saith the Lord. Thank you, Heavenly Father, for causing me to be successful in all my endeavors. I give you full control over my life to lead and guide me in an honest and respectable way. You are a present help in my time of need, so I will call upon you to teach me and give divine instructions. Thank you for allowing me to be the lender and not the borrower, above and not beneath, the head and not the tail in any situation. I thank you that your blessings are overtaking my life. Glory to your name! Amen.

GOOD SUCCESS

This book of the law shall not depart out of thy mouth,
but thou shall meditate therein day and night, that thou mayest observe to
do according to all that is written therein: for then thou shalt make thy way
prosperous, and then thou shalt have good success.
Joshua 1:8 (KJV)

We should keep the word of God in our mouths at all times. Doing so will lead and guide us into all truths. God's word is alive and powerful. It is sharper than any double-edged sword. His word can cut through our spirits and souls and through our joints and marrow until it discovers the desires and thoughts of our hearts. We can not fool God. He is all knowing, all seeing, and all powerful. He knows our inner thoughts, whether they are good or evil. We may not serve him as we should, but there is no getting away from him. My desire is that we reach out to God and develop a relationship with him before there is a crisis within ourselves.

Father, your word will always be in my mouth and in my heart. I shall study diligently so that I get an understanding of you, your character, and your love for mankind. I thank you for making my way prosperous and successful. I know that you are faithful in all your ways, and I want all that you have for me. You said in your word that you would never leave me or forsake me, so I am counting on you to bless, encourage, and create in me a right spirit. I declare that everything (land, money, personal possessions) the enemy has stolen from my family and me will be returned. Amen.

THE RIGHT CROWD

Don't ask me to leave and turn back. Wherever you go,
I will go; wherever you live, I will live. Your people will be my people,
and your God will be my God.
Ruth 1:16 (NLT)

Hang with the right crowd and the right people. Be careful of your surroundings. Watch out for the wolf dressed in sheep's clothing. The enemy comes to steal, kill, and destroy. But God has sent his son that we might have life and have it abundantly. Watch as well as pray. Watch who is constantly bringing you negative feedback about others. If they are quick to talk to you about other people, they may be quick to talk to those same people about you. Beware of the gossiping spirit. When you find a true friend, stay connected. True friendship is sometimes hard to find, but it is a precious commodity when you do.

Lord God, you are my God. Wherever you tell me to go, I will go. Whatever you tell me to do, I will do. I echo the words of Isaiah, Lord send me. I will dwell in your house. I will keep your commandments. The world has nothing to offer me because their way causes destruction. I will not be seduced by the trickeries of the world. Teach me to hold my peace and rebuild my life in silence. Send me great destiny helpers to be watchmen on the wall. Show me whom I am called to help. May I encounter you in the quiet of the day. May you speak to me in the dawn of the morning. May I see your goodness and majestic powers in the sunrise. Amen.

WORTHY GOD

I will call on the Lord, who is worthy to be praised: so,
shall I be saved from my enemies.
II Samuel 22:4 (KJV)

God is so trustworthy, dependable, and faithful. He is not like man. God is the same today, yesterday, and forever. We can always depend on him to see us through any trial or tribulation. When we are in pain physically or spiritually, God is the healer. We worship Father God for he is a present help. He is a way maker, miracle worker, promise keeper, and a light amid darkness. Man can be deceiving and undependable; therefore, we must continually call upon the Lord for all our needs. The world can be chaotic; therefore, we need a savior. God is a worthy God and worthy to be praised. He will save us from our enemies if we put our trust in him.

Father, I am calling on you because I have no other God to call upon. You are worthy of all praises. Protect me from the snares of the enemy. Keep me safe in your loving arms. You are my rock and in you will I trust. You are my shield and the horn of my salvation, my high tower, my refuge, and my savior. Keep me from all types of violence – domestic violence, gang violence, and spiritual violence. When my enemies seek to destroy me, you will cause them to stumble and fall. A thousand may fall at my side and ten thousand at my right hand, but none of them will come near me. I shall forever give you the honor, the glory, and the praise. You are a good God. Amen.

UNDERSTANDING HEART

Give therefore thy servant an understanding heart to judge thy people,
that I may discern between good and bad:
for who is able to judge this thy so great a people?
I Kings 3:9 (KJV)

Always pray for wisdom and understanding as King Solomon did in the Bible. He realized that these were the qualities he needed to be in the position of King over so many people. And because he did not ask God for wealth and riches, God granted him these things anyway. Let us learn to keep the main thing, the main thing. The scriptures say that if you do not have wisdom, then ask for it and, in all thy getting, get understanding. These two will carry you much farther in life than trying to accumulate material possessions to look successful. Wisdom and understanding will cause you to be a good listener. The fear of the Lord is the beginning of knowledge. And we all need knowledge. Seek first the kingdom of God, and everything you need in life will be provided for you.

Father, I thank you for the gift of discerning spirits so that I may discern good from evil. Thank you that the eyes of my understanding are open to see what you are showing me. I will look to you for answers. I will not jump ahead of you. I will not rely on my own understanding, but I will lean on you for everything. My trust is in you; therefore, I will take no thought for tomorrow because I know who holds tomorrow. Blessed be the name of the Lord. You are mighty, gracious, and amazing. I love you with all my heart. Amen.

PRAYING THROUGH

Go back to Hezekiah, the leader of my people. Tell him,
"This is what the Lord, the God of your ancestor David, says:
I have heard your prayer and seen your tears. I will heal you,
and three days from now you will get out of bed and go to the
Temple of the Lord."
II Kings 20:5 (NLT)

Pray through the situation, the circumstance, the illness, or the confusion that is in your life. It doesn't matter to God because he is the healer and problem solver of all. He heals our body, mind, soul, spouse, children, family members, neighbors, government, enemies, and any confusion or strife caused by the enemy. When God restores us from the attacks of the devil, we should show our appreciation by attending church, giving thanks and praise unto him, and being diligent servants. So many times, people get healed and restored, but then they forget who their deliverer was. After Hezekiah was healed, he went to church to worship God, and the Lord satisfied him with longer life. He followed the instructions of the Lord. We should also.

Father God, I thank you for your faithfulness. I thank you that you hear our prayers and answer our prayers. I thank you that you are all knowing and all powerful. Father, there is none other like you. We fail you miserably all the time, yet you still love us, protect us, heal us, restore us, direct us, and give us a good measure of life. We have been disobedient in so many ways. Please forgive us for our stubbornness. Father God, I thank you for being a promise keeper and a light in the midst of darkness. I am forever grateful. Amen.

OPERATE IN HUMILITY

If my people, which are called by name, shall humble themselves, and pray, and seek my face, and turn from their wicked ways; then will I hear from heaven, and will forgive their sin, and will heal their land.
II Chronicles 7:14 (KJV)

We should always operate in humility. If we call ourselves Christians, then this should not be a hard thing for us to do. Yes, sometimes we fall from grace, but we get back up and shake the dust off and kneel in prayer. We confess our sins before God, asking for forgiveness. None of us are perfect, but we serve a perfect God. He is always ready to hear from us. God is just a prayer away. Don't function in arrogance but have a modest and kind attitude knowing that you represent the God you serve. We must remember that the word of God tells us that pride leads to destruction, but humility leads to honor. Let us walk the road of righteousness, doing business in an orderly and decent manner.

Father, we ask for forgiveness for not heeding your call on our lives, for turning to the world's way of thinking in believing that the world has more to offer us. Forgive us father, for we have not done that which is right in your eyes. I repent on behalf of my family, friends, neighbors, and nation. I declare we will pursue your words of instructions. We will not go after other gods. We will not be disobedient. We will hearken to your voice and keep your commandments. We need you every day in our lives to lead us and guide us. Father God, you are our guiding light. Amen.

TELLING NO ONE

I slipped out during the night, taking only a few others with me. I had not told anyone about the plans God had put in my heart for Jerusalem. We took no pack animals with us except the donkey I was riding.
Nehemiah 2:12 (NLT)

Keep the God-given assignment to yourself! Often, we advertise what God has told us to do. He didn't tell us to broadcast the assignment. He wants us to ponder this in our hearts as we seek his guidance and direction for the next step. Once we announce the task that has been given to us, someone else may decide to go ahead and complete the undertaking because they are filled with envy of what you are prepared to do. But God did not speak to them; he spoke to you. I'm reminded of a desire to complete an assignment that would set me up for retirement. This desire was to open a Christian Book Store. I solicited help from another cousin to fulfill this desire. What I didn't notice was there was a lady across the room that overheard our conversation. Before I could finish the research for the endeavor, I received a call from this lady who told me that she was doing the exact same thing. As a matter of fact, she had everything completed and was ready for the grand opening. At first, I couldn't understand how this happened until I thought about that day at the bereavement visitation for my cousin.

Lord God, thank you for trusting me with your plan for your people. Continue to show me the different ways that I can be a blessing to all you have called me to be. Cause me to be silent and obedient. Order my steps in your word. Lead me on a plain path. Anoint me for the assignment. Give me your favor and favor with mankind. Send me great destiny helpers. Amen.

OBEDIENCE IS CRUCIAL

If they obey and serve him, they shall spend their days in prosperity,
and their years in pleasures.
Job 36:11 (KJV)

bedience (to the Lord) is crucial to our success and longevity. So, my question is, "Why wouldn't you serve the Lord God who is almighty?" If we heed his word, then surely goodness and mercy shall follow us all the days of our lives. If we obey and serve the Lord God, then longevity and success shall be our portion. I've seen countless people (some friends, some not) die prematurely, and I have often wondered what happened. I know the word of God says he will satisfy us with long life. So, did they ignore the voice of God? Did they operate in haughtiness? Or did they prefer to engage in what the world had to offer them? I choose to serve the Lord God.

Lord God, I will obey you all the days of my life. My ear is attentive to your word. Speak to my heart, Lord God. Let your will be done, not my will. I will be a voice to represent you to those who do not know you. I will intercede on your behalf. I will bring glory to your name. Father, use me to exalt you here on the earth. There is no other name I can call upon that would do me any good. Thank you for prospering me and giving me long life. Thank you for angels that keep watch over me. Father, you are so good to me. I am so grateful for your love. I will praise you forever. Amen.

MY PROTECTOR

The Lord is my rock, and my fortress, and my deliverer;
my God, my strength, in whom I will trust; my buckler, and the horn of my
salvation, and my high tower.
Psalms 18:2 (KJV)

God is a mighty rock, our protector, our refuge, and our hiding place. He is all-inclusive of whatever we need. When we are in trouble, he is the one to call upon. I am reminded of an incident when I was going to see my cousin who was very ill. I called her to tell her I was coming by after work. As I approached the house, I noticed her bedroom light was off. When I knocked on the door, a masked man snatched me into the house at gunpoint. He escorted me to the bedroom where my cousin was tied up on the floor. He and another guy instructed me to get on the floor as well. They took my keys and purse. While on the floor, I asked God to deliver me from the hands of my enemies, and he did. They took my new car and money out of my wallet and fled. God answered my prayer.

Lord God, you are my rock, my strong tower, my salvation. When the enemy tried to set a death trap for me, you delivered me. You help me with your victorious right hand. You covered me and protected me from hurt, harm, and danger. I am so grateful for your commitment to loving me. I can never thank you enough for your grace and your mercy. I will hide myself in you so that you will strengthen me as I go from day to day. I know you as a deliverer, a strong tower, and a shield of protection. Thank you for keeping me in your loving arms. I acknowledge you as the God of my strength. Amen.

MEDITATION OF HEART

Let the words of my mouth, and the meditation of my heart, be acceptable in
thy sight, O Lord, my strength, and my redeemer.
Psalms 19:14 (KJV)

Let your words line up with your heart. For out of the heart flows the
issues of life. Whatever is on your mind (whether good or evil) it will
sometime come out as you speak. It is so important to keep your heart
clean and diligent in seeking the will of God for your life. Without God's
guidance, the tongue can be very ruthless. The tongue carries the power of
life or death to a situation. Be careful what you say. People have often said
that God gave us two ears and one mouth. Therefore, be quick to listen
and slow to speak. Once we put those words into the atmosphere, they are
hard to retract. The demonic spirits will take those ugly words and cause
them to ring over and over in the ears of the person on the receiving end.
Demons love to hear nasty, hurtful, demeaning, and upsetting words. They
feed off this type of talk. On the other hand, if your words are kind, pleasant,
encouraging, and pleasing to God, you have been a tremendous blessing to
someone. God is smiling.

---

*Lord God, I need you to speak through my mouth and think through my mind. Father,
guide my tongue so that I may always speak on your behalf. For you are my strength
and my deliverer. Thank you for delivering me from the hands of the enemy. Thank
you for cleaning me up and causing my words to align with your purpose for my life.
Create in me a clean heart and renew the right spirit within me. Amen.*

STAND

Oh my God, I trust in thee: let me not be ashamed,
let not mine enemy triumph over me.
Psalms 25:2 (KJV)

Stand up for God because he is definitely looking out for us. We cannot be ashamed of the word of God. It is food for our soul. It is the manual for instructions and directions for life. It is the medical journal for any health issues one might have. The word of God has the answer for those legal issues that seem scary at times. It has the wisdom for all certifications to acquire employment at any level. It can help you fix your car, gadget, machinery equipment, or home improvement and give you divine training for the task at hand. God's word is all inclusive. He knows all, sees all, and is everywhere at all times. He is your healer, deliverer, restorer, banker, counselor, and way maker. That's who he is! Never be ashamed of this great God we serve!

Father God, I put all my unwavering trust in you. I depend on you for all my endeavors in life. I look to the hills from whence cometh my help because I know all my help comes from you Father. You, who made the heavens and the earth. You, who own the cattle on a thousand hills (meaning you own everything). For you alone have all the power to defend and protect me. Keep me on the straight and narrow path that I may continually exalt your holy and righteous name. Shield me from the tricks of the enemy. Cause my enemies to stumble and fall. Cover me in the day of trouble. You are my Lord and I put my faith in you. Thank you, Father, for being so merciful to me. I love you. Amen.

STRENGTH

Wait on the Lord: be of good courage,
and he shall strengthen thine heart: wait, I say, on the Lord.
Psalms 27:14 (KJV)

Strength is in the word of God because he will give you courage in the midst of the storm. If you are tired and weary, just rest in the Lord. Don't try to carry your burdens alone, give them to God because he is the burden bearer and heavy load carrier. You can trust him to handle the problem. People sometimes think they have strength without the help of God. They believe that they are self-made people. No one is self-made. God created all of us. When we learn to rest in the arms of our heavenly Father, life will be much better. This doesn't mean there will be no trials or tribulations. Rather, it means you will be equipped to handle those fiery darts of the enemy. The enemy will never get the best of you as long as you put your trust in God. He may not come when you want him to come, but God is always on time. He knows the end from the beginning. In other words, he is the master strategist. Wait on him and trust him, and he will strengthen you for the task.

Lord God, I am your servant. Give me the courage to do your will here on the earth. I will not go before you, but I will wait for your instructions. I realize my timing is not your timing. Give me rest from the weight I carry. Strengthen my heart. I know that your yoke is easy and your burdens are light. I will diligently seek you each day because I find peace and comfort in knowing that you are in control of my life. I patiently wait for your understanding and direction. Lead me, Lord God. Amen.

TROUBLE DON'T LAST

For his anger endureth but a moment; in his favour is life: weeping may endure
for a night, but joy cometh in the morning.
Psalms 30:5 (KJV)

Troubles don't last for always. Trouble has to leave when you are in the presence of the Lord. We all fall short of the glory of God, but we get back up. The enemy is treading on dangerous ground when he comes up against a child of God. God favors his children. He is our heavenly Father, and he knows our struggles. The earth belongs to God, but the devil will try to manipulate people into thinking he is the head. The devil cannot dwell in a holy place, so allow yourself and your surroundings to be holy. You seek God so that you train the next generation to seek him. Sure, we may have some downtime, but we serve a God who can lift our heads to a brighter day. Never give up! Keep on keeping on. God is your friend, and he loves you dearly.

Father, I know that I have done wrong things in my life that don't align with your word. I ask you for forgiveness. I have fallen short of your glory. I have not represented you well in the earth. I have not been a good ambassador for you. Cleanse me and wash me through and through. You and only you are the lifter of my head. Thank you for your favor that is over my life. I recognize that a brighter day is coming according to your word. I honor you Father, for you are great. I will praise you with my songs, words, and actions. I will walk worthy of the calling you have placed on my life. Amen.

WORSHIP IS A LIFESTYLE

I will bless the Lord at all times:
his praise shall continually be in my mouth.
Psalms 34:1 (KJV)

Worship is a lifestyle, not a Sunday morning hour session. We should reverence and adore God daily. He deserves our best. God is first and foremost in our lives. Each morning as your eyes open, your first words should be "Thank you Lord!" Don't forget that God is your source, so don't just give him lip service only. Give him sincere appreciation. Be a true worshipper. If you are a wolf in sheep's clothing trying to impress others of your religious status, then you are deceiving yourself. God knows your heart, and your heart is wicked. As you go through the day, there are so many things to give thanks for. When you step outside, you can see God's majestic wonders all around you. Think about who made the trees, flowers, grass, blue sky, fluffy clouds, the air you breathe, and so much more. We serve a magnificent God. He is the God of all creation. Everything you have is because of God almighty. Give him the praise that he so rightly deserves. God is our all and all.

Lord God, I will bless your holy name as long as I have breath in my body. For you are better than good to me. If I had ten thousand tongues, I could not praise you enough. I thank you for your goodness, grace, and mercy. I shall wear the garment of praise. I will praise you in the morning, noonday, and late at night. Your word will be hidden in my heart. I will sing a song of your greatness. I will exalt your holy name. Amen.

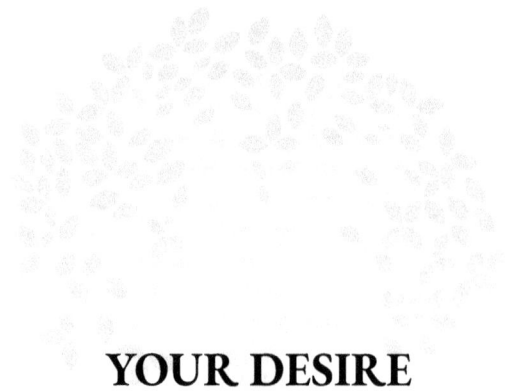

YOUR DESIRE

Delight thyself also in the Lord;
and he shall give thee the desires of thine heart.
Psalms 37:4 (KJV)

Your desire (of goodwill) is God's desire. Take care of God's business, and he will take care of yours. Do good unto others. Be kindhearted. Always be willing to lend a helping hand. Pray for others, even your enemies. Be mindful to always have an ear to hear what the Lord is saying. Allow him to lead and guide you in all decisions, circumstances, and situations. If you declare that he is the head of your life, then you must live that way. Give God the praise he so rightly deserves. Be thankful in all things, knowing that they are working for your good. Acknowledge God to be supreme. Follow his teachings. Be a good servant. Pray without ceasing. Know that he is God.

Father God, I take pleasure in knowing that you are the head of my life, that all my wishes, dreams and goals are aligned with your purpose for me. I am grateful for the many blessings you have bestowed upon me. You are a righteous God, and I love you dearly. I acknowledge your presence in my life. I bow down before you and not to the culture of this world. I reverence you in all areas of my life. You are my healer, my protector, my counselor, my everything. Father, I desire your word to come alive in me so that I may do your will. I am your vessel here on the earth. Speak to my heart and I will obey. Amen.

THE GOD LIFE

The steps of a good man are ordered by the Lord:
and he delighteth in his way.
Psalms 37:23 (KJV)

Lead a good God-ordained life and see how God advances your pathway. Stay in tune with him and you will not fail. Keep his word hidden in your heart and you will not fall. Sometimes in life, we tend to think we can do things on our own without the help of others and even God. We become self-serving and think that our education and community status is all that we need. We even forget where we've come from and how God has blessed us to get where we are today. Without the Lord on our side, we are nothing. But with God, we are more than conquerors. If we stumble, God is there to pick us up. No one is perfect but Father God. He loves us so much that he is with us at all times. He knows our humanity; therefore, he knows that the flesh can get weak at times. Nevertheless, he is a loving Father and wants nothing but the best for his children. Love him with all your heart and see the goodness of the Lord in the land of the living.

Lord God, I declare that I will walk upright before you. I will keep your commandments and I will do your will according to your word. You are my guiding light and I look to you for all my help. I will operate with consistent integrity as I am a representative of the Kingdom of God. I worship you only. I will put no other gods before you – not my family, job, finances, relationships, education, church, or businesses. Thank you for keeping me on the right track. I love you, Father God. Amen.

PATIENCE AND PRAYER

I waited patiently for the Lord;
and he inclined unto me, and he heard my cry!"
Psalms 40:1 (KJV)

God has your back – patience and prayer work really well together. God has delivered me from numerous incidents. He delivered me from the worry of this world, from family situations, from disruptive people, from past trauma. We don't get into these situations overnight, so we must wait upon the Lord to deliver us. God wants to know if he can trust us to not repeat that same thing. While we are waiting on an answer from God to rescue us, this is our time to pray to the Father acknowledging that he is Lord of our life. He is the lifter of our heads, and he will pull us out of the muddy and boggy clay that seems to have us stuck. We wait because his timing is not our timing. We wait because his thoughts are higher than our thoughts. God is sovereign, so there is nothing new under the sun to him. He knows what we need before we know. Some experiences are teachable moments, and some experiences are wake-up calls (calls to repent). When we get the call, we need to answer it.

Lord God, I relinquish my fears and anxiety over to you. I give you all my problems because they are too big for me to handle. You are the God that carries me through good times and not so good times. I know you are always with me. Thank you for being a mighty God, a just God, a faithful God. Amen.

TALKING THE RIGHT STUFF

Whoso offereth praise glorifieth me: and to him that
ordereth his conversation aright will I shew the salvation of God.
Psalms 50:23 (KJV)

Talking the right stuff is so important. Let your conversation be of a sweet aroma. Cause your words to be that of encouragement to others. When God is the center of your joy, people are happy to see you coming. Be dependable like your heavenly Father. Walk in the spirit of truthfulness and honesty. Don't be a hater, a back biter, and back stabber. The tongue is unruly and without the Spirit of the Living God inside of you, it cannot be tamed. The tongue will run wild; it can be boasting, bragging, cussing, intimidating, and downright nasty at times. With our tongues we should be a blessing to God our Father. People will use the tongue to curse others with sickness and diseases. The Bible tells us that death and life are in the power of the tongue. What are you speaking today? Is it a good God-ordained conversation, or is it a gossiping, derogatory discussion over someone's life? Be careful of the company you keep. Not everyone is a well-wisher.

Lord God, your praises shall always be in my mouth. I am a kingdom citizen. I represent you here in the earthly realm. I will study your word so that when I witness to others, they will be drawn to you and the universal church will be added to. Everyone needs you, Lord God. I will not be a part of idle gossip. You are my strength, my refuge, my shelter in the time of trouble. I place my life in your hands. I give you all of me. I ask you to mold me into your image. Thank you for shielding me from corrupt company with foolish conversation. Amen.

CLEAN HEART

Create in me a clean heart, Oh God;
and renew a right spirit within me.
Psalms 51:10 (KJV)

Cleanse us so that we serve you in a right manner. Wash us so that we serve you with purity, a right order, and with decency. Make our thoughts clean and pure. Sometimes we get out of step with you Father God and get mixed up with the wrong crowd. Lead us back to you. Don't let our enemy be victorious over us. You have been our help in days that have long passed and gone. You said you would never leave us or forsake us. Purify us from the inside out. We want to live a life of holiness because we serve a Holy God. If we have offended someone without knowledge, direct us back to them so that we can get it right. We desire to operate in the right spirit – your spirit. We will keep your word hidden in our hearts and not talk out of both sides of our mouths. We will not be double-minded people. We will walk upright and carefully, always giving you the highest praise – hallelujah. We bless your holy name.

Heavenly Father, search me through and through to remove anything that is not like you. Search me oh God, and know my heart; try me, and know my thoughts. If there be any wickedness or evilness in me, cast it out. I repent of all sin – known and unknown. Give me a clean heart so that I may proclaim your holy spirit to the multitudes. Cleanse me from all the unrighteousness and wickedness that tracks the earth. Thank you for being a forgiving and righteous God. I commit my ways unto you. Use me for your glory. Amen.

EVERYDAY PRAYER

As for me, I will call upon God; and the Lord shall save me. Evening and morning, and at noon, will I pray, and cry aloud: and he shall hear my voice.
Psalms 55:16-17 (KJV)

Prayer is so important for our everyday well-being. We go to the doctor to stay well. And that is good because God gave us these professionals for that purpose. When we choose a physician to be our caregiver, we should pray about which one to select. Not all doctors are believers. Not only are they not believers, but some have some ungodly attributes. I am reminded of an incident with my sister. She called me about helping her select a gynecologist. Upon her visit, he found a spot on the mammogram. She had the surgery and attended the therapy that followed. She decided to go back to her primary care physician. She told him what had happened since her last visit with him. He told her that this wasn't news to him because he had already detected that over a year ago, yet he wasn't the least bit concerned about her having the cancer. Especially since he knew over a year ago and did not tell her. This is why you should pray about everything, and I mean everything. Call on the Lord. He will hear you and save you from destruction and stumbling blocks that man will deceitfully put in your way. Pray, pray, pray!

Lord God, I will continuously seek after you. No matter what time of day it is, I know that I have the right to consult with you, to praise you, and to always give thanks to you. For I realize you hear my every petition, and I am so grateful. I will cry unto you Lord God, and you will rescue me from the snares of the enemy. Amen.

THE SANCTUARY

Until I went into the sanctuary of God;
then understood I, their end.
Psalms 73:17 (KJV)

Do not let the wicked discourage you. They are always up to some no-good deed. In life it looks as though the ungodly prospers more than the godly. But there is an ending for those who acquire material possessions by deceiving others. Be careful because they look good on the outside but have wicked hearts. They will even try to recruit you to be part of their wicked empire. Don't question yourself or think you're not doing the right thing when you see them boasting and boiling about what they've got. When God elevates you, then you will be on the right track to prosperity. Wealth and riches shall be in your house because the wealth of the wicked is being laid up, right now, for the just. God has justified you, making you in right standing with him. Material goods are treasures that will fade away, but your relationship with your heavenly Father is eternal life. David said he didn't understand this until he went to church and heard the word preached. The word was that the ungodly destination would not be heaven. Then he understood.

Lord God, I have had some good days and some not so good days, but through it all, I knew that you were near. The days and the nights seemed to get longer and longer without any justice. Then I went to church, and I heard the word of the Lord. Your word breathed life into me and set me on a straight path. I am forever grateful for you. Your word is a lamp unto my feet and light unto my path. Lead me and guide Lord God. Amen.

THE SECRET PLACE

He that dwelleth in the secret place of the
Most High shall abide under the shadow of the Almighty.
Psalms 91:1 (KJV)

The enemy can't touch you – you're in the secret place. I love to hide in the secret place of my God. The secret place is when I shut the naysayers, the gossipers, and the envy watch dogs out. Just basking in the presence of the Most High God is a beautiful experience. As much as possible, we should consecrate ourselves before the Lord. Shut out all the noise and chatter. We should be reading the word of God and praying for wisdom and understanding. This will give us clarity, anointed strategies, and revelation knowledge. Being in the secret place heightens our awareness and gives us keen discernment. God is speaking in the secret place. He's giving divine instructions and directions. We are safe in his arms, and he desires to hear from us. Speak God, speak. Your servant patiently awaits to hear your voice.

Lord God, I surrender myself unto your will for my life. I commit myself to your word and to your work. Use me Lord for your glory so that I may be a blessing to the people of God. I acknowledge your presence, your power, and your authority. I will sanctify myself in your presence so that I may hear from you. I will put the world behind me, and I will look to you for guidance and direction. You are my shelter, my protection, and my refuge. I am in awe of your unwavering love. You are my anchor. I will hold onto your unchanging hands. Thank you, Lord God, for allowing me to reside in the secret place. Amen.

LONG LIFE

With long life will I satisfy him and show him my salvation.
Psalms 91:16 (KJV)

God has declared long life for us. But will we walk in his word? Seldom do people read this verse or if they do read it, I wonder if they really trust the word of God. So many times, we predict a self-fulfilling prophecy by speaking the wrong thing over our life. I once heard a young lady jokingly talk about her grand uncle who always said it was better to die young to avoid the aches and pains that come with age. This is a self-fulfilling prophecy. Others might say that a certain type of sickness or disease is in their bloodline, so they actually expect to get it. Or when they do get it, they are complacent because their great-great-grandma had it. This is not what the word of God tells us. God said to call upon him when we are in trouble, and he will answer us and deliver us. Then he will honor us with long life. If we abide in him, he will abide in us. Live a life so close to God that when others see you, they will first see God in you. He will hold you up with his victorious right hand.

Father, I receive your word of long life for me and for my family. I will live according to your word. I will have good intentions toward all mankind. For I know the plans you have for me Father, plans of peace and success. Thank you for loving me and directing me in all my endeavors. Thank you for delivering me from the hands of the enemy. I praise you and love you. You are my refuge and my fortress. I put all my trust in you. Thank you for hearing me and answering me. Amen.

BLESS THE LORD

Bless the Lord, oh my soul: and all that is within me, bless his holy name. Bless the Lord, oh my soul, and forget not all his benefits" Who forgiveth all thine iniquities, who health all thy diseases;
Psalms 103:1-3 (KJV)

God is a healer, he's our redeemer, he's forgiving and merciful. We should bless his holy name every day because every day is a new day with new blessings. His benefits are numerous. To name a few: he gives us good health, favor, prosperity, grace, abundance, strength, increase, right connections, authority over the enemy, mercy, divine revelation and strategies, open doors of divine opportunities, and so much more. We cannot forget that God is almighty and can do anything we need him to do. However, we sometimes fail to call on him. Don't be afraid. God is waiting to hear from you. God knows we live in a body and the flesh gets weak occasionally. He still forgives us when we repent and turn away from that wickedness. He heals our bodies from sickness and diseases. We will bless him daily. We will praise his holy name. We will acknowledge his goodness.

Father God, I thank you for being the great physician, healer, my sustainer, and protector. I will honor you and give you all the praise for you are a mighty God. Thank you for being a keeper and a forgiving God. I take authority over every stronghold that is trying to attack my body, my finances, my family, my job, and all that concerns me. Whom the son sets free is free indeed. I command sickness and disease to leave my dwelling. You are my healer and deliverer. I love you, Father God. Amen.

THE SENT WORD

He sent his word, and healed them,
and delivered them from their destructions.
Psalms 107:20 (KJV)

God has a plan for your health. And there is no distance in the word of God. If you are praying for a friend or family member that lives many miles away, fret not because God's word can travel like the speed of light. I can remember as a little girl a minister in our community would occasionally call my mother to have prayer with her. In those days there were no speaker phones. However, her prayers were so intense you could hear her praying while mother held the phone to her ear. If you cannot physically get to the person to pray with them, then give them a call and have prayer. People need deliverance and they need to be restored to God's way of living. Many people are sick because of the lifestyle they lead. There is a great need for the teaching of God's word to many. We perish for lack of knowledge. Staying in tune with God is healthy – it is good physical health and good mental health. God loves all of us, and he wants us to walk in good health. But if we don't know this or know him, we can get into a lot of trouble. God is the healer.

Lord God, I realize that prayer can see no time or distance in the spirit. As I pray for those that are afflicted, I thank you for sending your word to heal and deliver them all. I thank you for hearing my prayer and for answering my prayer. Lord God, you are the great physician. There is nothing too hard for you. When trouble comes, you are a deliverer. You are the great I AM. I trust you with all my heart. Thank you for your greatness. Amen.

THE BLESSED LIFE

Praise the Lord! How joyful are those who fear the Lord and delight in obeying his commands. Their children will be successful everywhere; an entire generation of godly people will be blessed. They themselves will be wealthy, and their good deeds will last forever.
Psalms 112:1-3 (NLT)

Reverence the Lord at all times, so the blessing of the Lord will be upon you and your family from generation to generation. How wonderful is that! This is the summation of a blessed life. If you fear the Lord, which is to respect, honor and worship him, then you are at a good place in your life. Because of this, you will keep and obey his commands. You will be upright, honest, and decent in all your dealings with others. This blessed life will follow your children because you have set an example of a godly life before them. Then their children will be blessed because the family has been taught to honor God and his word. Success and blessings will cause your family to operate in the overflow. You will hearken to the voice of the Lord and relish his commandments. Grace and mercy will follow you. You will be a blessing to your community because you love and trust the Lord.

Father, I thank you that my children are blessed and highly favored by the Lord. Thank you, Father, that they are protected and successful in all endeavors. Thank you that the blessing goes from generation to generation. I realize that the fear of the Lord is the beginning of wisdom. I honor and obey you, Father God. I am in awe of your goodness, generosity, and kindness. Your praises shall constantly be in my mouth. Amen.

GOD'S BEST

This is the Lord's doing; it is marvelous in our eyes. This is the day which the
Lord hath made; we will rejoice and be glad in it.
Psalms 118:23-24 (KJV)

God wants the best for all of us. He is a loving and kind God. When
trouble hits, God will rescue us. When times seem dark then the light
comes; it is the work of the Lord. It is his doing because he is so gracious to
us. We depend on God rather than on people. People will change, but God
never changes. He is the same today, yesterday, and forever. God is merciful
because he blesses us even when we don't deserve the blessing. Each day is
a new day that God gives us new opportunities, favor, grace, and strength
to endure. What a wonderful blessing. As our eyes open each morning, we
give thanks to our Almighty God. It is another day that he has blessed us and
kept us. He didn't have to do it, but he did because he is good. We delight
in his goodness and give him the glory and the honor for he is in our life.

---

*Lord God, this is the day that you have made, and we are so grateful to be part of it.
We celebrate this day of life, and we thank you for it. We realize that there's nothing
that we've done to deserve it, but it is your grace and mercy that have allowed us to
see another day. We reverence you for all your goodness. Your mercy endures forever,
and we are forever grateful. When the enemy tried to take me out, Lord, you were
there to make him stand back and behave. When trouble seems to be on every side,
Lord, you were there to lift me up to a higher place of peace. Lord God, you are my
shelter. I will rejoice in your goodness. Amen*

THE HIDDEN WORD

Thy word have I hid in mine heart, that I might not sin against thee.
Psalms 119:11 (KJV)

Keep the word of God at the forefront of your heart and mind. We often forget that we are not in charge. We accomplish some things in life, and we feel as though we have arrived and that we don't need anyone else. Life can be tricky like that, but we must keep our hands in God's hand if we want success to continue. Many people put their trust in their money. But when the business collapses and the so-called friends are gone, we are left holding the empty bag of sorrow. Business, home, credit, spouse, and friends have all vanished. Instead of seeking wise counsel from God, people rely on their status to see them through. The enemy will allow you to ride high for a season; then he drops the bomb. This has been such discouragement for so many people who thought they had it all together. Life has many obstacles and hurdles to jump over. We need God to direct our track so that we stay on the right course. When God is at the head of the game of life, you can't lose. The word of God is so powerful that it can help us channel through any hindrances that may appear. Keep the word in your heart; you won't go wrong.

Father, I am determined to study your word because I know it is life to my bones. I know that your word gives me understanding, revelation, and insight. Therefore, I will keep your word in my heart so that I will be a blessing to all I encounter. I will pray your word back to you because I know you will honor it and cause it to perform. Thank you for your word. Amen.

THE EVIL PATH

I have refused to walk on any evil path,
so that I may remain obedient to your word.
Psalms 119:101 (NLT)

Beware of the company you keep; it may be more harmful to you than good. The enemy will disguise himself. He is very cunning and sneaky. He will imitate God's people just to gain access into your environment. The enemy will make you feel as though he is your best friend. He loves to go to church and pretend to be a worshipper. He is even a member of several ministries. This is how he gets a foot hold on the congregation, and before you know it, he has caused all kind of confusion. If the church is not spiritually strong, the enemy will cause a split or shut the doors. It is vitally important that God's people pray for the gift of discerning spirits. This gift will allow us to distinguish good from evil. You will know the fake people immediately and you will refuse to co-habitat with them. Once they know that you recognize who they really are, they will try to discredit you. Keep your distance and remain steadfast and unmovable, always abounding in the work of the Lord. God will direct your path, and you will know that your work is not in vain.

Father, I thank you that you are ordering my steps that I may do that which you have ordained. Keep me grounded in your word. I command the enemy to stand back because he has no place in my life or the life of my family. I take authority over every evil plot of the enemy and declare every plan of the enemy be made null and void. I bind the demon of destruction, deception, and distraction. I will be obedient to your will and your way. Amen.

THE WORD IS A LAMP

Thy word is a lamp unto my feet, and a light unto my path.
Psalms 119:105 (KJV)

God will light up your pathway so that you can see clearly. You will know where you are going and what you are needed to do. You will walk in clarity according to the word of God. God will go before you and break up all unproductive ground. He will make every crooked lane straight, cause rivers to flow through the dry desert land, and make every valley experience a smooth one. He is the God of impossibilities. You can do all things through him. He will cause your enemies to be your footstool. They will flee from you seven different ways. God charts the way for us because we don't always know which direction to take, but we can depend on God to give us divine direction. He will give us love, power, and a sound mind. If we follow his word, he will free us from sickness, disease, worry, condemnation, ungodly soul ties, rejection, poverty, evil spirits, witchcraft, intimidation, and manipulation.

Lord God, thank you for making a way in the wilderness. Thank you for being the God of breakthrough. Thank you for making ways out of seemingly no way. You are my light and my salvation, and in you I will trust. Your word directs me and comforts me. You know the end from the beginning, so I put all my trust in you. I thank you for your wonder-working power. Thank you, Lord God, for being that bright guiding light. When I don't know which way to turn, I turn to the rock that is higher than me. You are my rock. Thank you for divine instructions and divine directions. Lead me and guide me, Lord. Amen.

MY STEPS

Order my steps in thy word:
and let not any iniquity have dominion over me.
Psalms 119:133 (KJV)

Lord, we need you to lead us and not let these evil inclinations control us. The flesh is weak so we must be diligent in God's word. The word of God will cause us to not stumble along the way. All our help comes from the Lord. He made the heavens and the earth and all that is within. He is our deliverer, and he will rescue us from the hands of the enemy. People will say that they want to be led by the Lord but then decide to follow their own selfish desires. God cannot deal with a double-minded person. You are either hot or cold: hot for the things of God or cold for the things of the world. Trying to have it both ways will only bring confusion. So much disturbance, pain, and sorrow are the results of people trying to serve two gods. We go to church on Sunday to be spiritually fashionable. But when Monday comes, we are different people. I once heard about a lady who attended a holiness church with a strict dress code – no pants. She worked in a factory and before she would go on the floor, she would change into jeans for work. At the end of the day, she would change back into her long skirt. It seems as though she was serving two masters.

Father, I pray you will lead and guide me in your word. Give me insight and revelation knowledge, and open doors of opportunity to serve you at a higher level. Thank you, Father, for divine order, divine insight, and divine foresight. I take authority over every evil tendency that will try to attack me. I cast it down, and I send it back to the pit of hell. I worship you and only you. Amen.

DELIVER ME

Consider mine affliction and deliver me:
for I do not forget thy law.
Psalms 119:153 (KJV)

Lord, you know our situation, please deliver us from the hand of the enemy. He comes to steal, kill, and destroy. He wants to steal your joy, kill your body, and destroy your legacy in the earth. The enemy does not want you to have a good life, a comfortable life, or a life filled with the word of God. He wants to steal your ability to have prosperity. He tries to keep you in poverty – living from paycheck to paycheck. The enemy wants God's people to be sick, hurt, worried, in turmoil, mentally ill, confused, and traumatized. He wants to kill your body and your dreams. He loves when people speak evil against you. His demons feed off wicked conversations contrary to the word of God about you. The enemy tries to destroy everything God has already ordained for your life. He wishes to see you in a state of ungodly addictions, being involved in evil spirits such as lying, seducing, and believing in witchcraft more than you believe in God. The enemy wants to destroy everything that is good in your life. He is the destroyer.

Father God, deliver me from every affliction, every flaw, every tactic, and every scheme of the enemy. I honor you with your word. I will keep your commandments and I will hearken to your voice so that I will be blessed coming in and blessed going out. I bind every plot and plan of the enemy to do me harm. I cast down every hindering spirit that comes against me. Thank you, Father, that everything I put my hands to is blessed. Amen.

LOOK TO THE HILLS

I will lift up mine eyes unto the hills, from whence cometh my help. My help
cometh from the Lord, which made heaven and earth.
Psalms 121:1-2 (KJV)

Lord, we look to you for help with everything because you are our
source, our resource, and our supplier. You have given us both good
health and a strengthen body. You have given us breath with clean air to
breathe. You have given us eyes to see, ears to hear, and mouths to speak.
You have given us a sound mind with great intelligence. Every era of life,
you increase the wisdom of mankind. You are a strategic and progressive
God. You know man's limitation, so give us what we need when we need
it. With every generation, the round of grace goes higher and higher. We
look to an all-powerful and all-knowing God because you are our help in
times of trouble, discouragement, sadness, confusion, sickness, distraction,
and deception. We understand that all our help comes from you. You never
slumber or sleep. You watch over us with an unconditional love.

---

*Lord God, thank you for being my everything. Thank you for being all mighty, all
knowing, and everywhere at all times. God, I can always call on you because you are
always nearby. I look to you for all answers because everything that was made was
made by you. I realize that all my help comes from you, and I can do nothing without
you. You have not given me the spirit of fear, but of power, love, and a sound mind. I
will follow your teachings. I will trust your word. You are my keeper, my refuge, my
strong tower. Hold me in your hand. Amen.*

THE HAND OF THE LORD

The Lord will perfect that which concerneth me: thy mercy, Oh Lord, endureth
forever: forsake not the works of thine own hands.
Psalms 138:8 (KJV)

Put it in the hands of the Lord and he will take care of it. There is nothing
too hard for God. Our anxiety is sometime overwhelming because
we try to handle problems all by ourselves. We must learn to cast our cares
upon the Lord because he cares for us. We worry too often about things
we have no control over. There is opportunity for stressful conditions in
so many areas of life – work, family, church, friendships, various events,
government, relationships, and life in general. We particularly gain anxiety
over church hurt. This can be devastating to the believer. Because people
are "in church" does not necessarily mean they are "in God." People go to
church for various reasons. Some go to find a spouse, while others go to
seek a leadership position. Other members may be those who had a mean
spirit when they joined the church and still have that same spirit. They tend
to have a sharp tongue hurting others' feelings and not apologizing. If you
cross paths with these so-called members, you may run into an unkind word
because they are on a mission. And their mission usually ends disastrously.

---

*Lord God, I give you my problems, my insecurities, and my fears. I bask in your
presence. I know the plans you have for me, plans to do good for me and cause me
to be successful. Thank you, God, that you let the enemies that rise up against me be
smitten before my face and flee from me. You are a great God. Bless be the name of
the Lord. I love you, God. Amen.*

SEARCH ME

Oh Lord, thou hast searched me, and known me. Thou knowest my downsitting and mine uprising, thou understandest my thought afar off.
Psalms 139:1-2 (KJV)

The Lord knows and sees everything. There is no hiding from him. It is so important that we realize this as we go through life. People think because they can't see God with the naked eye that he does not exist and therefore they don't have to respect him. This is incorrect thinking. We see God's marvelous work every day. The trees and flowers did not plant themselves. Who put the sun, moon, and stars in the sky? Surely man cannot take credit for that. God knows everything about us. He even knows what we are going to do before we do it or what we're going to say before we say it. He knows our thoughts from afar. No need to hide when you find yourself in a dilemma. Talk to your heavenly Father, he is near. He desires to hear from you. God will never lead us into mischief. But if we get caught in harm's way, he always has a way of escape for us. He is just good like that, and we should reverence, respect, and give him praise each day.

Lord God, you are so amazing! I thank you for your greatness. I am in awe of your majestic powers. You know my every move, so I ask you to lead me and direct me on a righteous path. I bless you and honor you. Thank you for being a way maker. When I can't see my way, you've already made the way. Glory be to God! I am forever grateful for your compassion and goodness. Blessed be the name of the Lord. Amen.

BROKEN IN HEART

He healeth the broken in heart, and bindeth up their wounds.
Psalms 147:3 (KJV)

The Lord hears your heart's cry. He sees your brokenness. Things don't always go the way we perceive. Life happens and we find ourselves in a position of loneliness. Something we have worked so hard for has disappeared. It is no longer there, and we feel abandoned. Our spiritual heart is broken. This could be the loss of a loved one through divorce or death. It could be that the job closed after several years of your hard work and dedication. Either way, there is a void that needs to be filled. And the one to fill it is God Almighty. As he fixes our brokenness, he gives us rest and peace to carry on. God has limitless strength to cover us and enough spiritual bandages to wrap us up tightly. He is the master of all things. Sometimes a doctor's report can put us in an unhappy state of mind. We feel betrayed, discouraged, and sad. Our heavenly Father knows exactly what we need when we need it. The Great Physician can fix any problem that arises in our life. We must learn to give our brokenness, sadness, rejection, and even anger to him. We cannot allow these hindering spirits to manifest in us, causing more pain and misbelief. We give it to God, and he will do the healing.

Lord God, sometimes my heart is so heavy. But I know you are a healer, so I give you my problems, my brokenness, and my struggles. Send your ministering angels God to encouragement me. Give me the desires of your heart. Open the understanding of my eyes so that I may see what it is you are doing in this season of my life. Thank you for healing me and restoring me. I will forever give you the praise and the honor. Father, you said vengeance is yours and you will repay. Amen.

ACKNOWLEDGE HIM

Trust in the Lord with all thine heart; and lean not unto thine own
understanding. In all they ways acknowledge him,
and he shall direct thy paths.
Proverbs 3:5-6 (KJV)

Reverence and admire the Lord in all that you do. This should be everyone's reasonable duty. The Lord has done so much for all of us. We should give honor where honor is due. The alarm clock did not wake you up this morning. Your money cannot buy you heavenly peace. Your good looks will not be the channel for you to get into heaven. In other words, we've got to ask God for understanding and revelation knowledge. College cannot give us the education that the word of God can give us. We thank God for schools and educators. Just as we thank him for doctors and attorneys. He placed them here to help us and they do the very best they can. We pray for them. We ask God to cover them with his infinite wisdom. Before we go to the best school, doctor, or lawyer, we pray a hedge of protection over ourselves and them. We all need God. Don't think you know everything so that you don't need anyone. The greatest manual and book of instructions is the Bible. It gives us wisdom, understanding, and long life – a life that is well lived.

Lord God, I come before you with a humbled heart and hands of thanksgiving. I put my trust in you because you are a faithful God. I cannot make this journey without you. I need you, Lord God. Thank you for salvation. Thank you for revelation knowledge, insight, and wisdom. I honor and trust you with my life. I delight in your word. Thank you for ordering my steps. Glory be to God. Amen.

THE PRINCIPAL THING

Wisdom is the principal thing; therefore, get wisdom:
and with all thy getting get understanding.
Proverbs 4:7 (KJV)

We all need wise counsel occasionally, and who better to gain this from than God himself? I worked a temporary assignment for approximately five months. The person training me was going on maternity leave. I was to be trained for three weeks because this was a highly sophisticated accounts payable system I would be using. The person decided to leave just after two weeks of training to go on her extended maternity leave. I took notes every day because there were at least 21 steps per sales order. When she abruptly decided she was not coming back that next week, I was terrified. I was told the system cost one million dollars – again terrified! As I drove home that day, I had a talk with God. I said "God, if you don't show me how to work this system, I don't know what I will do." And I was very serious because I didn't feel competent to use it by myself. However, I took my notes out the next day and I followed the steps I had written. Within a few weeks, I didn't even need my notes. I couldn't believe it, but I remembered my talk with my God. He gave me the wisdom and understanding to get the job done.

Father God, I ask you for wisdom and understanding because you said it is the main thing that I need to function in life. It will guide me into the right places with the right people. Thank you for giving me wisdom and understanding at such a crucial point in my life. You are the Great Counselor. Amen.

INCLINE THINE EAR

My son, attend to my words; incline thine ear unto my sayings. Let them not depart from thine eyes; keep them in the midst of thine heart. For they are life unto those that find them, and health to all their flesh.
Proverbs 4:20-22 (KJV)

Good health is in the word of God. The word of God feeds our soul, spirit, and body. We are a three-part being so God's word is relevant to all three parts. I wouldn't be here today if I hadn't made the word of God a part of my daily life. As a young bride, four months into marriage, I was sick unto death. The doctors could not pinpoint the cause of the illness. Thank the Lord I had some praying family members who sought the counsel of the Almighty God on my behalf. It was my mother's uncle who first decided that we needed to go beyond the report of the doctor. Whose report would you believe? We believed the report of the Lord. Within a week or so I began to feel better. My weight was down to 90 pounds , and I had no appetite. God heard our cries, and he answered our prayers. There is a healthy life in the word of God. A daily dose of the word will keep you in perfect peace because your mind is stayed on him. The enemy is always seeking to take us down, but God always has a way of escape for his children. Allow the word to penetrate your heart.

Glory be to God! My health is found in the word of God. Lord God, I declare that I will follow your word – to do your will. I will study faithfully to gain insight for a healthy body, healthy relationships, and healthy outcome in all my endeavors. Thank you for allowing me to have access to your word. Amen.

A DILIGENT HEART

Keep thy heart with all diligence; for out of it are the issues of life.
Proverbs 4:23 (KJV)

From a clean heart will flow clean words. Whatever is in a person's heart is usually what will be spoken. It is important to think before we speak. If we are angry, then the wrong tone and words will be spoken. This causes strife and controversy among people. We are then deemed as judgmental to others. God is the judge of all. We cannot always say what we think or feel. When we keep our heart clean, we refrain from idle talk, gossiping, lying, and being double-minded. Our hearts should be attentive to the word of God, allowing God's word to lead us. The word of God is a biblical road map for life. It keeps us on a straight path, ignoring all the world's carnal distractions. The enemy is waiting for us to let our guard down so that he can run rampant with one little idle word spoken or indulging in the wrong conversation. My husband told me about this deacon who always sat in his car at work to eat his lunch. He very seldom ate with the rest of the team. I knew then that he didn't want to engage in meaningless conversations with the other guys. He wanted to guard his heart and keep it clean.

Father God, I surrender my mind, my heart, and my will to you. Use me for your glory. I ask that your will be done in my life and not my will. Speak through my mouth and think through my mind as I am your vessel here in the earth. Cleanse me from all unrighteousness. I honor you, Father God. Amen.

ESTABLISHED THOUGHTS

Commit thy works unto the Lord, and thy thoughts shall be established.
Proverbs 16:3 (KJV)

Be obedient to the word of God and live an abundant life. Abundance is our inheritance and our portion. Our church celebrated its 125th church anniversary one year. My husband was the committee co-chairman. The chairperson had family issues and could not coordinate this event. So, the pastor asked my husband to step up to chair. This was a huge undertaking to say the least. It was a three-day event with a Friday night banquet at the local country club, a community cookout on Saturday at the church, and two services on Sunday. The committee was a great group to work with. But even with a diligent hard-working committee, you never know how the crowd will be. After all our meetings and careful planning, we still prayed and hoped that it would be a success. Arriving early that Saturday morning, I began putting things into place. After a couple of hours of working, I was called to the front to do an interview with a local newspaper. When I finished talking with the reporter, I walked through the church to the back yard to continue setting up and, to my amazement, the entire yard was full of people. I was astounded to see so many church and community people in the yard. It was totally amazing. Our efforts and diligence had paid off. We committed our work to the Lord, and he definitely established our way. It was a grand occasion to remember.

Lord God, if I follow your will for my life, I realize I can't go wrong. For there is no wrong in you. You are a holy God and I bow down before you. I reverence you in all my actions. I commit myself to doing your mighty works. Amen.

PLEASANT WAYS

When a man's ways please the Lord,
he maketh even his enemies to be at peace with him.
Proverbs 16:7 (KJV)

Serving the Lord has its benefits. Church folk can truly be pieces of work. There is a difference in just going to church and really having God in your heart. People come to church for various reasons that are not spiritual. When you encounter these church goers, you have to see them for who they are. They usually like to be seen and thought of as very intelligent. They pretty much carry a chip on their shoulder because they think they are smarter than most people. When they offend you and you have done nothing to them, they actually wait for you to apologize to them. They will wait for years for your apology or your presence around them. How arrogant is that! Eventually, they will make their way into your company and give you a round-about apology. It is never "I am sorry." They will talk around the subject but never really repent for the error of their ways. Again, they are too important to make a mistake, so they won't truly acknowledge the offense. But they want things to be just as they want them to be. You don't have to do anything when you are confronted with these people. God has already paved the way. He gives you the victory because your enemy has to bow.

Heavenly Father, thank you for giving me peace – peace of mind and peace in the midst of a storm. I denounce worry and aggravation. You are the great counselor, so any concerns I have I will give them to you. I will not allow the enemy to intimidate me. Thank you for your grace upon my life. Amen.

HAUGHTY SPIRIT

Pride goeth before destruction, and a haughty spirit before a fall.
Proverbs 16:18 (KJV)

When we allow the flesh to rule, we fail tremendously. Our egos can get the best of us sometimes when we leave God out of the picture. Any attempt to accomplish a dream or a goal you have set for yourself will not succeed if you put God on the back burner. He must be the head of all ventures in life. God gives his people wonderful, successful opportunities and they forget about him and lose it all. When the wealth is evident, they begin to spend money like it is a free product. They get really lavish with gifts, trips, and parties. They forget about family and the ones that helped them when they were ordinary working people. Their ego is inflated, and they see the world as a playground. Their children are neglected because they are too busy being the big shots in their circle of friends. Then one day it is all gone: the business, the spouse, the children, and the so-called friends. This is a hard fall from the grace of God. The fleshy thoughts and ideas will destroy a good business, marriage, and family. But God is good because if you repent and turn from your wicked ways, he is just to forgive you and heal you from what you thought the world owed you. Have a humble spirit.

Lord God, I bind, rebuke, and pull down every haughty spirit operating in my life. I will not engage in prideful acts or unhealthy tendencies. I will not have a high-minded attitude toward others. Lord God, create in me a clean heart and renew your spirit within me. I will treat my neighbor as myself. Thank you for ordering my steps. Amen.

SPEAK LIFE

Death and life are in the power of the tongue:
and they that love it shall eat the fruit thereof.
Proverbs 18:21 (KJV)

Speak life (positive thoughts) into all situations. See the good in everything instead of the worst-case scenario. The Bible tells us that the tongue is unruly and needs to be tamed. It can be tamed by reading and studying the word of God. Allowing God's word to fall into our heart will cause our words to be covered with a sweet aroma. We speak from the heart. When a drunk person tells you something that may be hurtful to you, that's because the person has gained enough courage to tell you exactly what they think of you. It's in their heart, but they are afraid to say it when they are sober. Guard your heart with persistent prayer and searching of the scriptures. Let your conversation be good fruit, music to the ear, and life to those who hear it. There is an old cliché that says you can catch more flies with honey than you can with vinegar. Who wants to be around a sour mouthed person? Of course, no one does. People prefer the sweeter conversations because they encourage and lift up your demeanor.

Heavenly Father, I speak life into my family, friends, neighbors, church family, co-workers, government, and all who I encounter. I pray blessings upon our nation and other nations. May everyone I interact with be filled with your glory. May a hedge of protection be around them. May they want for nothing, and their houses be filled with plenty. I thank you Father for your goodness and your mercy. Amen.

WHERE IS YOUR VISION

Where there is no vision, the people perish:
but he that keepeth the law, happy is he.
Proverbs 28:18 (KJV)

We can die spiritually and physically without the word of God. A spiritual death is horrible because a person has lost their zeal for the things of God. They have turned away from his word and decided to do life on their own terms. They feel as though they don't need God and they start on a journey of destruction. This journey could cause a physical death. We perish for a lack of knowledge, knowledge of the word of God. The word of God is everything to us; it gives us life, direction, instruction, good health, wisdom, understanding, prosperity, long life, favor, and salvation. The Bible is our guidebook for life. We should read it and ask God for understanding. God is gracious and merciful. He forgives us of our sinful characters when we repent and turn away from the wrong lifestyle. I am reminded of hearing about a man who was at a club one night on the dance floor. He got hot and stepped outside to cool off and fell dead. That bothered me because I wondered if he had a chance to pray a simple prayer. If he did, I know God heard him.

Lord God, your word shall forever be in my mouth. I thank you that the Word of God is a compass that helps me in my daily endeavors. I lean and depend on you God for direction, understanding, and knowledge. You are my heavenly guiding light, my daystar, and my sunshine on a cloudy day. I will continually seek your wisdom for my life. I thank you for revelation knowledge. Amen.

BEAUTY DOES NOT LAST

Charm is deceptive, and beauty does not last;
but a woman who fears the Lord will be greatly praised.
Proverbs 31:30 (NLT)

You can't get by in this world with just beauty. You need a relationship with the Lord. So many young ladies believe that the beauty pageant will get them where they want to be in life. Sometimes there is a price to pay on the beauty queen trail. We have heard of too many horrible stories in the news lately of how this has turned out. Beauty is a gift from God. But your inside beauty is far more important than your outside beauty. Because you reverence God, people will notice the beauty you carry inside. Doors will open for you. Success will be your portion. God will delight in you and show you favor. The outside beauty will last for a season, but the God-fearing beauty will be with you forever. When the vain beauty is gone, the notoriety and friends are gone. But the respect-of-God beauty will be with you when the friends are long gone. And this beauty will go from generation to generation. Your children will know how to view tomorrow because they know who holds tomorrow. This is a generational blessing.

Heavenly Father, there are so many things in this world that are deceiving. I ask you to keep me on the straight path that always leads back to you. I admire you; I am in awe of you. You are amazing! Your praises shall forever be in my mouth. I reverence you in all things because my trust is in you. Thank you, Father, for your graciousness and kindness. You are a merciful God. I love you. Amen.

THE WHOLE DUTY

Let us hear the conclusion of the whole matter: Fear God, and keep his
commandments: for this is the whole duty of man.
Ecclesiastes 12:13 (KJV)

Make sure you get the whole story before making any kind of judgment.
We are sometimes too quick to judge others. We don't have the
facts and we assume, which is guess work. In a court of law there are many
testimonies to hear before the jury can make a reasonable decision. This can
take days because the jury and the judge want to be accurate in the sentencing
of the crime. They don't assume anyone is guilty without fair due process of
the case at hand. Let us hear the entire account of the matter. Don't be so
quick to throw people under the bus because they might get run over. Our
job is to give reverence to God and obey his word. If we can manage to do
that, then we can live a clean life. Judging others is not our responsibility.
God is the ultimate judge. He has the last word. Our opinion is how we view
the situation without any facts. We once had a Sunday School teacher who
would always give us her opinion of the lesson. This frustrated me because
I wanted to know what the word of God was saying, not her opinion. She
would give us her opinion on life and what she thought church folk should
be doing. She would never characterize the lesson and make it relevant to
life today. Just her opinion.

*Heavenly Father, let the words of my mouth and the meditation of my heart be
acceptable in thy sight, Oh Lord, you are my strength and my redeemer. I ask you to
guide my tongue, allow me to be a good listener, and not make judgement on others.
I will respect and obey you. Amen.*

EVERY WORK

For God shall bring every work into judgment, with every secret thing,
whether it be good, or whether it be evil.
Ecclesiastes 12:14 (KJV)

Remember, we all must stand before God to give an account of our deeds. The day I stand before God, I cannot give an account for my husband, my children, my grandchildren, my siblings, or any other person in my life. I can only give an account of what I have done, whether it is good or bad. He will not ask me about others, only me. Sometime people will try to hide their sins from mankind as if man can grant them salvation. There is no need to pretend before man because God sees all. And God will judge us for everything we have done, even the things done in the dark that people think no one knows about. It is time out for the wolf dressed up in sheep's clothing. The wolf thinks he is deceiving all the people in church, but he is not tricking God. The wolf loves to come to church and hide its sinful nature and pretend to be someone else engaging people in conversation just to get in their business. The wolf is destructive and will scheme to get its way in the church. This is a hindering spirit in the church, and it needs to be dealt with. The wolf deals in manipulation.

Heavenly Father, I come before you with my needs in one hand and my wants in another. Asking you Father to forgive me for backsliding, for being dishonest, unjust, and unethical. I know you see all, and you know all so I bow before you in humility repenting of my sins that are ever before me. Give me a clean heart and upright spirit so that I may serve you in truth and in righteousness. I surrender to you. Thank you, Father. Amen.

THE GOOD LAND

If ye be willing and obedient, ye shall eat the good of the land:
Isaiah 1:19 (KJV)

If you are willing to follow the promises of the Lord, then plenty shall be your portion. My husband and I often talk about growing up in the rural part of the county. We reminisce about how our parents would prepare in the summer for the winter months. A big garden was planted and vegetables were canned or put in the deep freezer. The deep freezer was an additional freezer either in the house or in the shed outside. Certain vegetables were not canned or frozen, such as sweet potatoes and white potatoes. The sweet potatoes were housed in a bank – a bank of dirt that looked like a mound or small hill. The white potatoes were kept under the house in a layout spread. During the fall of the year, a farm animal would be slaughtered, and the meat would be packaged in the freezer. All winter we ate the good of the land. Our parents were willing and obedient so that they could provide for the entire family during the winter months. If we are willing and obedient to follow God's word and keep his commandments, then we will walk in abundance. This is what God desires; he desires that we have an abundant life. Surrender to him and he will cleanse you from all unrighteousness.

Lord God, I will keep your commandments and seek after you each and every day. Your promises are yes and Amen. Therefore, I will not rebel against your word. I thank you for the grace to trust, believe, and receive from you. You are a mighty God and I love you dearly. Thank you for bringing me into a good land. Glory be to God. Amen.

PERFECT PEACE

Thou wilt keep him in perfect peace, whose mind is stayed on thee:
because he trusteth in thee.
Isaiah 26:3 (KJV)

Staying in line with God's word will bring peace in the midst of a trial. A trial can sometimes be a testing of your faith. God needs to know that he can trust you in good times as well as not so good times. When my husband and my son both had heart surgery four months apart, I probably would have lost my mind if I didn't know God. It was a very trying time for me to say the least. But I trust God. My relationship with my Lord gave me the strength to endure. There were days when I cried, but I didn't give up. I had to be strong for them. I didn't realize that God had already prepared me for this journey. I was a part of a prayer band at church. We met every Saturday for prayer at 12:00 p.m. at the church. It usually lasted three hours. That same group would go out into the community during the week to pray with those who were sick, scheduled for a hospital stay, or homebound. Occasionally we would go to more than one house, not getting home until midnight. We also made visits to the hospitals and the nursing homes. God had strengthened my prayer life so that I could encounter a certain level of peace in the midst of the storm. Stay focused on God; he's your shield.

Lord God, I thank you for perfect peace – peace that surpasses all understanding. I lay my burdens upon you because you are a burden bearer and a heavy load carrier. I will seek you all my days because my faith is strong, and my mind is committed to your way and your will. Thank you for unmerited favor. Amen.

STAND

The grass withereth, the flower fadeth:
but the word of our God shall stand for ever.
Isaiah 40:8 (KJV)

The flowers and the grass may dry up, but the word of God is eternal. I love God's green earth. In the summertime the grass is so green and beautiful. It looks like a green blanket across the land. The flowers compliment the grass with their variety of colors. Spring and summer are my favorite seasons because I get to plant flowers and see the beauty and majestic wonders of the Lord. The things that we grow are seasonal, but God's word is forever. God is forever – he will never leave us. When we plant a seed, it comes up and it may not. Sometimes we have to plant a second time. The birds may eat the seeds, or they may eat the plant as it starts to grow. But the word of God is the same today, yesterday, and forever. It is important that we accept the word of God, believe it, and hide it in our hearts so that it speaks back to us. We need the word of God to point us in the right direction. Life can be complicated so we need God's divine direction. He will guide us through the small and big conditions. We should study, meditate, pray, and rest in his presence.

Lord God, I thank you for continuously being there for me. I know that I can always count on you no matter what the situation is because you are there. I call upon you sometimes in the midnight hour and you hear my prayer. I give you my problems and my struggles, and you are an on-time God. You have rescued me from the snares of the enemy. And I am so thankful. What a mighty God you are! Amen.

WINGS OF EAGLES

But they that wait upon the Lord shall renew their strength;
they shall mount up with wings as eagles; they shall run,
and not be weary; and they shall walk, and not faint.
Isaiah 40:31 (KJV)

Weariness is not the end, keep on keeping on because God has your back. Don't get tired in well doing. We can't run ahead of God. He is progressive and strategic. He knows the end from the beginning. Waiting on God is your prayer, fasting, and meditation time. He has not forgotten you; he is working behind the scenes. Just be still and know that God is working on your behalf. The songster said, while we are trying to figure it out, God has already worked it out. Patience is an advantage because it gives you time to surrender totally to God. Let him know you cannot handle the situation, but he can. You understand the greatness of God, so you relinquish your troubles to him. He is the one that will walk you through while giving you the strength to endure. You will come out spiritually stronger, wise as an eagle, and physically capable to handle the next challenge because you know who holds your future. We can always lean and depend on the Lord to see us through no matter what the condition might be. God is faithful and his mercy endures forever.

Heavenly Father, thank you for making me stronger for the battle. I will anticipate your every move. Give me guidance and divine direction. I will not be exhausted in well doing; but I will continue to give you the honor and the glory for your majestic powers. Thank you strengthening me. Amen.

WOUNDED

But he was wounded for our transgressions,
he was bruised for our iniquities: the chastisement
of our peace was upon him; and with his stripes we are healed.
Isaiah 53:5 (KJV)

The Lord has taken away our sicknesses and diseases, our troubles, and bad acts. He has given us his best gift – his beloved son. There is no greater love. When we accept the Lord into our life, we accept what he has done for us. We accept everything he paid the price for so that we may live an abundant life. He has given us free will, good health, peace, revelation knowledge, understanding, wisdom, doors of opportunity, divine instruction, and direction. He does not make us choose him because he wants us to come freely. Healing is ours if would just accept it. A Godly life is a healthy life. Your health and your healing are in the word of God. The enemy will place wicked trials in our way causing us to stumble from time to time. But God is a good God, and he will not leave us or forsake us in the time of trouble. Our job is to reverence and trust him. He loved us and knew us before we were formed in our mother's womb. He cares for us. No one else can do for you like God almighty. Seek him today.

Father God, just like bad children before a good daddy, you are so gracious to us. Thank you for not leaving us but giving yourself as a ransom for us. I am eternally grateful for your depth of love that you have for us. I cannot comprehend what you have experienced on our behalf. Father, I thank you for all you do. You are amazing! Amen.

NO WEAPON

No weapon that is formed against thee shall prosper; and every tongue that shall rise against thee in judgment thou shalt condemn. This is the heritage of the servants of the Lord, and their righteousness is of me, saith the Lord.
Isaiah 54:17 (KJV)

People may try to bring you down, but you belong to the Most High God. Weapons will be formed, but they won't manifest. So many people, many claiming to be my friend, have tried to put obstacles in my way: weapons of jealously, envy, hatred, malice, witchcraft, backbiting, backstabbing, intimidation, and manipulation. People I thought I could trust were not who they pretended to be. And the sad part about it is that the majority of them were so-called Christians. As I have mentioned earlier, there is a difference between the Christian and the church goer. My problem was that I used to take people at face value. Meaning, however you presented yourself to me, that was who I perceived you to be. I had to learn at any early age that not everyone who is nice to me necessarily likes me. This has been very discouraging throughout the years, but I've learned to distinguish the good from the evil. Sometimes when God sets you apart, others will resent you even the more. I knew it was really bad when my former pastor's wife wrote this verse on a strip of paper and passed it to me in church. She saw the resentment.

Heavenly Father, I just want to say that I love you for who you are. You are great, worthy, faithful, amazing, and so much more. You bind the tongues of the ungodly and you cause judgment to come against them. You are a righteous God, and I walk with you. Thank you, Father for your faithfulness. Amen.

HIGHER GROUND

For as the heavens are higher than the earth, so are my ways higher than your
ways, and my thoughts than your thoughts.
Isaiah 55:9 (KJV)

You are not smarter or more powerful than the Lord. And until mankind realizes this, there will always be division among God's people. God has given mankind so much wisdom and, in most cases, man does not reverence God for this gift. So many people think that they are self-made intellects. They want to rule the world. God made the entire universe, and he is in control. Man will never be able to take God's position. This type of thinking comes about when man leans to his own understanding. We cannot leave God out of our daily lives. When we get so educated that no one can tell us anything, we are headed for a fall. We should humble ourselves under the mighty hand of God, and he will always show us what to do, when to do it, and where to go to get it done. God's word produces good, peace, joy, and prosperity. His word is reliable. I advise you to live by it.

Lord God, I adore you for your greatness, your faithfulness, and your eternal love for me. I will always look to you for answers, suggestions, direction, and instructions for my daily living. You are almighty and all powerful, so I surrender my entire existence to you. I put all problems in your hands because you can handle it when I don't know what to do or where to turn. Thank you, God, for being the holy God that you are. I give you, my life. Use me for your glory. Amen.

MY COVENANT

And this is my covenant with them, says the Lord. My spirit will not leave them, and neither will these words I have given you. They will be on your lips and on the lips of your children and your children's children forever.
I, the Lord have spoken.
Isaiah 59:21 (NLT)

It's a great thing to know that the Spirit of the Lord lives on and on from generation to generation. Blessed be the name of the Lord! As parents we should be the best mentor for our children. We should be the best witness for the Lord that they have seen. If we train them to love and respect the word of God, then we have given them a firm foundation. The word of God is in our heart and in our mouth. We speak life into every situation bringing peace and joy. Our words carry power because the spirit of the Lord is upon us. Our children are blessed because we have taught them the word of God. We have demonstrated God's power before them. We have taught them how important it is to have a dedicated prayer life and a relationship with God. We have displayed the blessings and miracles of God before them. They will teach their children and their children will teach the next generation. It is a generational blessing to know the Lord.

Heavenly Father, thank you for your word that will live with me and my children and their children forever. Your word is so powerful. It is life to my soul. I need your word everyday as I grow closer and closer to you Father. Thank you for this precious gift. It will not depart out of my mouth. I declare your word will always be in my bloodline. I will forever serve you. Amen.

I KNEW THEE

Before I formed thee in the belly I knew thee; and before thou camest forth out of the womb I sanctified thee, and I ordained thee a prophet unto the nations.
Jeremiah 1:5 (KJV)

Isn't it good to know that the Lord knows everything! He knew us before we were even conceived. That really blows my mind. It tells me just how powerful and majestic God is. There is no one else like him. He is superb. And he has good plans for our life. He tells Jeremiah that he has proclaimed him to be a prophet to the nations. What has God called you to do? He has great plans for all of us, but we keep running away from him. We have no discipline when it comes to following God. We stray away often and, in some cases, never come back. It's like a bad marriage. One spouse continuously runs away from home and then returns every time to find the welcome mat laid out. We run away from God, and he always accepts us back just as we are. No strings attached. No tricks and no gimmicks. He is so loving and gracious. When we fall, he's there to pick us up. When we stray away from his teachings, he welcomes us back with loving open arms. God has plans for us to have a healthy life, a successful life, and a purposed driven life. We are purposed to do his will. He is an intentional God.

Lord God, you knew me before I came into this world. I owe you everything – my life, my work, my belongings, my mind, and all that concerns me. I am forever grateful for the love you have for me and for how you have orchestrated my life. I ask that you continue to guide me. I love you, Lord God. Amen.

OBEY MY VOICE

But this thing commanded I them, obey my voice, and I will be your God, and ye shall be my people: and walk ye in all the ways that I have commanded you, that it may be well unto you.
Jeremiah 7:23 (KJV)

Obedience brings a good life. I cannot stress enough how important it is to obey God's word, to listen for his voice and to walk in his ways. Just like you obey the supervisor on your job, you must obey God. My first job out of college was at a nuclear power plant. I was hired as a clerical associate. When the supervisor would leave the premises, the other ladies would huddle and talk. I didn't know them that well, so I continued to work. One of the other supervisors always walked by at that particular time and speak to everyone. What he was doing was watching us. I didn't realize that at the time. I was promoted from clerical associate to clerk stenographer to office manager. My supervisor was the office manager. I got her job! She explained to me how pleased she was that I didn't stop working when she was out of the office to get in the crowd and talk. Doing what I was hired to do caused me to advance rapidly. The moral of the story is, you never know who is watching. Do your best and be your best because God has good plans for you.

Father God, I will be obedient to your will and to your way. I will listen for your voice. I will ask for understanding so that I may complete my assignment. I know that obedience is better than sacrifice, so I yield my life to you. Thank you for giving me a plan of instruction for a good life – obedience. Thank you for being such a compassionate and praiseworthy God. Amen.

THE PLANS

For I know the plans I have for you, says the Lord. They are plans for good and not for disaster, to give you a future and a hope.
Jeremiah 29:11 (NLT)

The Lord wants only the best for his children. He is the best, so he wants us to have the best. Have you ever consulted God on what you should be doing about a particular situation? Try it, he has the answer. I have been awakened in the night hearing God tell me to pray for these people. I said, "Okay God, who is it you want me to pray for?" As he gave me the names, I began to pray. Prior to 911 happening, I was instructed by God to pray for police officers. I didn't know what geographical area I was to pray for, so I prayed for all police officers. Then 911 happened and we were all devastated. As the news unfolded, I notice quite a few fire fighters were killed in the rescue attempts. I asked God why more fire fighters died than police officers. His answer was that whoever he had petitioned to pray for fire fighters did not heed the assignment. Often God will just speak right back to you. Again, I was shocked, but glad I was obedient. Have you been called to be an intercessor? God has good plans for you.

Lord God, thank you for the righteous plans that you have for my life and for always leading and guiding me in a divine direction. Thank you, God, for desiring the very best for me. I don't deserve it, but you are so gracious and loving. I love you, Lord God. I will continually give you all the honor and all the praise. You have been better to me than I could be to myself. Lord God, you are the best. I love you. Amen.

RESTORATION

For I will restore health unto thee, and I will heal thee of thy wounds.
Jeremiah 30:17 (KJV)

Divine healing comes from the Lord. Our obedience, commitment, and attentiveness to the word of God is crucial in living a spirit-filled healthy life. Many years ago, early in my marriage, I had been prescribed medication for my stomach. Life was stressful, as expected being a new bride and mother with a new job. Then one day a rash appeared on my face and my mouth. It seemed to get worse, so I made a doctor's appointment. After a careful examination, the doctor said he was taking me off the medication. He deemed that I was allergic to it. He did not prescribe any other meds. As we were going home, I told my husband that I was somewhat uncertain about not having the medicine for my stomach. I was in doubt that I could do without it. I felt a little terrified. My husband immediately told me that I didn't need the medicine because I was healed according to my faith. I looked at him in amazement. I asked if he really thought so. He said, "Yes, you are healed because of your deep love and loyalty to God."

Heavenly Father, I feel so broken sometimes but your word tells me that you will restore me and heal me. I am forever grateful for your tender loving kindness toward me. I know that you are the great physician and that there is nothing too hard for you to do. I give you my body and my mind to heal from all the distraction of this world. Walk with me and speak to my heart. You are my loving Father. I honor you this day. Amen.

GOD OF ALL FLESH

Behold, I am the Lord, the God of all flesh:
is there anything too hard for me?
Jeremiah 32:27 (KJV)

There is nothing too hard for the Lord. He is omnipotent, which is almighty and all powerful. So, rest assured that he is very capable of handling any problem you might have. At times God has allowed jobs to actually look for me. When I was unhappy at one particular job, God caused my friend to call me because her sister worked in the Human Resource Department at a local business and knew of an executive opening that needed to be filled quickly. I was hesitant, but I went online and completed the application. Needless to say, I got the job. God can cause money to come to you when you least expect. At times you may be getting low on funds and wondering how you are going to make that little bit last. And just out of nowhere, someone comes by and blesses you with a monetary gift. God is just good like that. He takes care of his children just like your earthly father would do. There is nothing too difficult for God. If sickness attacks your body, remind God of his word. He said we are healed by his stripes. His word will not return to him void.

Lord God, I acknowledge that my sins are ever before. Wash me with your word so that I may be a good steward upon the land. There is nothing too hard for you Lord God, so I ask for your grace to be upon my life to direct me in godly manner. Thank you for being the God of all flesh because everyone needs you. You are awesome, amazing, wonderful, and so incredible. What a mighty God you are. I love you. Amen.

CALL UNTO ME

Call unto me, and I will answer thee,
and shew thee great and mighty things, which thou knowest not.
Jeremiah 33:3 (KJV)

God holds the keys to greater ways of obtaining success and prosperity. He knows the secrets to the good life. He has the medicine that the doctor does not have. He knows strategies that the smartest person you know cannot even figure out. God is so powerful that when you show up for the battle, your enemy has already been defeated. The enemy gives us fear, but God gives us peace. As I stepped up to the microphone as the worship leader one Women's Day ceremony, I was trembling inside something terrible; but when I opened my mouth, the word of the Lord took over and I was as cool as a cucumber. He showed me that day that he was an on-time God and that he is a deliverer. I had been praying for weeks about that assignment but did not hear anything from the Lord. He just showed up and showed out. The answer to my prayer had been concealed until the appointed time. Trust and obey is the key. Some would say "do it scared." Whatever you decide, know that God is there.

Father God, you have given me everything I need as it pertains to life and godliness. I thank you for being a great and mighty God. Thank you for giving me that I need and want. You are so generous and liberal in your giving. All I do is call upon the name of the Lord. This is so rewarding and satisfying to know that my heavenly Father acknowledges my requests. Thank you, Father God, for hearing my prayers and for answering my prayers. You are a great God and greatly to be praised. Amen.

HOPE AND WAIT

It is good that a man should both hope
and quietly wait for the salvation of the Lord.
Lamentations 3:26 (KJV)

Hoping and waiting patiently as the Lord works on our behalf. God is not to be rushed. He operates on his timing. He delights in our patience knowing that we fully trust in him. Some people try to run ahead of God and complete the task on their own terms. This was not good for Sarah and Abraham as they tried to jump ahead of God's promise. Hope is having an expectation and confidence that God will do what he said he would. Hope builds our faith as we allow our patience to work. God delivered me from the hands of the enemy when I was robbed at gunpoint. I waited on the floor, tied up execution style while the gun men rode off in my brand-new car. I needed deliverance, but I wasn't going to get up off that floor until I was pretty sure they were gone. I waited patiently for the Lord, and he heard my cry.

Father God, all my hope is in you. I gently wait for your instructions. Redeem me from all unrighteousness. Deliver me from the hands of the enemy. I put my trust in you. You are a faithful God, so I depend on you to lead and guide me in a right way. My salvation is in you, Father God. You are everlasting and the eternal God. Your love for me is timeless. Thank you for your infinite wisdom and never-ending passion for a wretch like me. I don't deserve all you do for me, but I am so glad you love me. I delight in you. You are the joy of my soul. Amen.

A NEW HEART

A new heart will I give you, and a new spirit will I put within you: and I will take away the stony heart out of your flesh, and I will give you a heart of flesh.
Ezekiel 36:26 (KJV)

We receive the spirit of the living God so that we walk upright and carefully acknowledging him with every step. He is imparting his spiritual genetic character into us so that we look and act like our heavenly father. Some people are so hard-hearted toward others. They are not happy with themselves; therefore, they are not content with the rest of the world. They have a controlling spirit. They will manipulate and intimidate everyone and everything around them. These people do not care who they hurt. From history we have learned that some rulers of other nations have been so hateful that they've allowed innocence people to be killed in war times. It does not bother them if women and children are killed. They are heartless and cruel. God wants to give them a new heart and a new spirit.

Heavenly Father, my heart is vexed with ungodly thoughts and deeds. Clean me up Father, for I know I am tirelessly undone. I have run in the wrong direction long enough. I surrender to you. I need you in my life. I repent of all the ridiculous, sinful, and immoral things I have done. You know my thoughts and they are not worthy of your presence. Please give me a new heart, a passion, and excitement for life. Take away everything that is not like you, Father. I shall be forever grateful to you for a loving and gentle spirit. Lead me in the right path. I will give you the honor and the glory forever. Amen.

MY STRONGHOLD

The Lord is good, a stronghold in the day of trouble;
and he knoweth them that trust him.
Nahum 1:7 (KJV)

The Lord keeps us stable when trouble comes. There is no need to fret because God is our refuge, our fortress, and our deliverer. Wicked people will do wicked things because their hearts are evil. God is slow to anger. He even gives the wicked time to repent. Sometimes they wise up and sometimes they don't. But we who love the Lord and trust in him have a safe haven. God is our protector and our provider. He safely guards us in times of trouble. He shields us from the awful deeds of the enemy. God gives us wisdom and understanding to maneuver through the plots of the devil. The enemy wants to take us out, but God has a shield of protection around us. As long as we stay prayed up, studying the word of God and meditating on the goodness of God, the enemy has no jurisdiction over our territory. Please be careful to not let your guard down. Don't leave an open door for the enemy to come in; that is, through strife, envy, jealously, mean spirit nature, deception, and the like. If you leave a portal open, the wicked one will seize the opportunity to reap havoc in your life. Keep your life surrendered to God. He will protect you.

Lord God, thank you for your protection over my life. Thank you for the dawning of a new day. Deliver me from my enemies, for they are ever before me. Keep me in a safe place, a secret place, a holy place. Shield me from all danger. Cause my adversary to flee. Restore my soul for my confidence is in you God. Take charge of my life. Give me a new start. Amen.

MAKE IT PLAIN

And the Lord answered me, and said, write the vision, and make it plain upon the tables, that he may run that readeth it.
Habakkuk 2:2 (KJV)

Follow the vision the Lord has given you, write it in everyday language. Journaling can be very helpful and sometimes very therapeutic. God gives us ideas, dreams, and visions. It is always a good idea to jot down what he is saying at that particular time. I have notes from years ago. When the time comes, God will reveal to you what he wants you to do with the information. Keep a tablet by your bed on the nightstand because he speaks in the night season also. Don't sleep on him because he does not sleep on us. God has much to say, so keep your ears tuned in to his voice. These messages are for an appointed time that God has chosen for you to release. You can trust what God has in store for you in the future. Don't allow doubt to come into your heart. Be obedient to the voice of the Lord. Your chosen time is near, though you may have to wait, it will be established.

Heavenly Father, give me insight and revelation knowledge so that I may know the times of the seasons. Invade my dreams to expose plans you have for me. Order my steps for a great outcome. Cause my hands to bless everything they touch. I will write the vision on the tablet of my heart. I will keep your instructions close. I will be obedient to do your will. Thank you, Father, for the life-giving guidelines that will cause me to operate in your grace and be fruitful in the land. I love you, Father. Amen.

CONSIDER YOUR WAYS

Thus, saith the Lord of hosts; Consider your ways.
Haggai 1:7 (KJV)

Are you following the word of the Lord or are you following your own thoughts? Stop and take a good look at your life. How does it compare to the word of God? It may represent the things you have built rather than the glory of God. We sometimes have great ambitions that drive us to work hard to become the best in the business. Then, we boast and brag about what we have done. Never acknowledging God in any of the process. I once saw a movie about a drought in the land. All the crops were failing, and the farmers were devastated. The devil approached one farmer (in disguise) and asked if he wanted it to rain on his crops. The farmer said, of course. So, it rained on his land and his fields were reaping much harvest. His barns were full of grain and his livestock had plenty to eat. His wife had a baby boy and life was really good...or so he thought. Until one day, the devil appeared to him and asked how things were going. The farmer said that everything was wonderful. The devil told him it was time to pay. The farmer was puzzled as he asked the devil how he should pay him. The devil told him the payment was his newborn son. He explained to the man that he does not give something for nothing. As the movie ended, the farmer was screaming and crying, "No, no, no!"

Lord God, I worship you and I adore you. I bow down before you. Teach me your principles. Do not let me fall by the wayside or cause my enemies to devour me. Help me to stand firm on your word. I will not put man or possessions before you. I love you, Lord God. You are worthy of all the praises. Amen.

WHOSE INFLUENCE

Then he answered and spake unto me saying,
this is the word of the Lord unto Zerubbabel, saying, not by might,
nor by power, but by my spirit, saith the Lord of hosts.
Zechariah 4:6 (KJV)

Remember: It is not your influence that gets the job done. One of the most widely buzzing words of today is "influencer." Everyone wants to be connected to an influencer. They believe that this person can make the right things happen for them. As a matter of fact, they believe this person can take them to the next level. All this is good if you have found a godly influencer. One who knows the Lord, respects, and loves him. Influencers have connections, talent, and are very creative. However, your true dependence should be on the almighty God. He is the ultimate influencer. Man can help tremendously, but he is no match for God. You can't force achievements without the right ingredients. So, it is not your strength that gets the job done. But rather, it is by the Spirit of the Lord. Let him breath on your project.

Father God, you are almighty and all powerful. I can do nothing without you. I depend on you. You are my God. My strength comes from you. You will deliver me from all hurt, harm, and danger. You will protect me in the times of disaster and tragedy. I lean on you because all my help comes from you. I will seek after you daily. I will inquire of your goodness, your integrity and righteousness. You are the Lord God who is all powerful, who possess strength and influence. I reverence you, Father. I am in awe of your mighty works. Thank you for not leaving me. Amen.

DIVINE ORDER

And I will rebuke the devourer for your sakes,
and he shall not destroy the fruits of your ground;
neither shall your vine cast her fruit before the time in the field,
saith the Lord of hosts.
Malachi 3:11 (KJV)

God shall restore divine order in your life. The devourer has to stand back when you diligently seek God. When your spiritual life is in order, the enemy can't pull you down. The weapon may be formed against you, but it will not manifest. When we take care of God's business, he will take care of our business. The lyrics to one of my favorite songs sum it up: I walk with God and every day he's walking by my side and he promised that he would be my guide. And oh, if you trust him and never doubt him, he will surely bring you out. Why he's the key to my success and I walk with God. I heard this short song one time in church, and it has always stayed with me. Walk with God.

Heavenly Father, thank you for taking control of the enemy and for not allowing him to consume or overwhelm me with grief. Thank you that all is well and that I have plenty for myself and for my family. I adore you Father because you are a good Father. You take care of your children and for that I am grateful. You could have left me in the wilderness of life, but you are so gracious that you picked me up out of a pit and place me in a good land. Thank you for causing harmony and peace to be my portion. I am forever grateful for your divine insight. You cause rivers to flow in the dessert. You are the God of breakthrough. Thank you for your compassion, mercy, and grace. Amen.

GOOD WORKS

Let your light so shine before men, that they may see your good works, and
glorify your Father which is in heaven,
Matthew 5:16 (KJV)

How bright is your light shining? Make sure it is shining so bright that others will see God in you before they actually see you. An old spiritual song title was "Let the Work I've Done Speak for Me." You are an ambassador for God. You represent him in the earth. Be a good steward of God's word. Don't be a lover on Sunday and a hater on Monday. This is a bad witness and could cause others to fall because they were following you. Lately, in the news we have seen generals in the faith take a nosedive due to hidden sin. This can be devastating to the body of Christ. It is so vitally important that we establish a relationship with Christ for ourselves. Instead of following man, we follow our Lord and Savior, Jesus Christ. That way, we will be an encouragement to others by being a good witness, thus causing the universal church to grow. So many people are searching for true believers. Will you be one?

Heavenly Father, I will glorify you daily so that others will see you through me. I will speak of your kindness, your generosity, and your good works. Use me as your vessel, your ambassador, your representative here in the earth realm. Anoint me to teach others so that this world will be a better place. I declare unity among the nations, among families and among the body of believers. I exalt thee of God. I adore thee. I magnify your name. Amen.

TWO MASTERS

No one can serve two masters. For you will hate one and love the other;
you will be devoted to one and despise the other.
You cannot serve God and be enslaved to money.
Matthew 6:24 (NLT)

We are constantly trying to leap over the fence. We want to do it our way. Instead of following God's principles, we want to make our own rules. Money does not wake you up in the morning. It is not a healer. It cannot restore you. It is not eternal. So why does mankind love money so much? Some allow money to substitute God because they think they are safe with lots of money in their possession. There is no salvation in money. Money cannot buy you a seat in heaven. People want prestige and status too often while they are here in the earth, but that will not get you a seat in the kingdom. Put your trust in God almighty and not in money. Look to the one who created money. Your money may fade away, but the word of God shall stand forever. God shall supply all your needs.

Father God, you are Lord of Lords and King of Kings and I honor you this day. I put no other god before you. You are my all and all. You know my thoughts from afar. You know my down sitting and my uprising. I surrender my life to you. You are creator of everything. Father God, I thank you for being all knowing, almighty, and everywhere at the same time. You are majestic, awesome, amazing and revelatory for such a time as this. I see the world changing all around me, but nothing can separate me from your love. Thank you for being a glorious God. I love you, Father. Amen.

JUDGE NOT

Judge not, that ye be not judged.
Matthew 7:1 (KJV)

Stop talking about others! Don't speak condemnation over people. Having a critical spirit and a self-righteous attitude will only raise chaos and eventually cause destruction. When we are critical of others, we are saying that we have it all together, that we don't make any mistakes, that we are near perfect. This is a hypocritical approach to life. No one is perfect but God himself. He sits high and he looks low. He sees all and knows all. So, he will do the judging. It is sometimes interesting that people will try to get the speck of dust out of your eye when they have a large board in theirs. How can one be so condemning of others when their evil doing is all in the street? God said don't judge, because one day you will be judged.

Heavenly Father, I come before you as humbly as I know how, asking you to cleanse me and forgive me for any and all wrong I have done against my sisters and brothers in Christ. You are the high priest, the king, the judge, and I come before your heavenly court to present my case for forgiveness. Thank you, Father for allowing me to plead my case before you for I know you are a just God. Thank you for being a good listener and a fair judge of character. I will not speak ill of others. I will not condemn my sisters and brothers, nor will I think less of them. For I am no better than them and we all belong to you. Give us a heart of thanksgiving that we may dwell together in unity. You are my Lord and my Savior. I will trust and obey you. Amen.

YOUR DESTINY

Ask, and it shall be given you; seek ye shall find; knock,
and it shall be opened unto you.
Matthew 7:7 (KJV)

Your destiny is in your mouth! Wow, what a mighty God we serve. Ask and keep on asking; seek and keep on seeking; knock and keep on knocking and the door will be opened for you. God is so faithful, and he hears our cries. When I was a young child, my parents owned a night club that was left to the family. They would get home, where I would be with my cousins, very late at night. It was so frightening because our house was not close to any other house in the neighborhood. As I went to bed, I would pray, asking the Lord to have my parents stop with the night club. I kept asking God, kept seeking his will, and kept knocking at the door of his heart. After a few years, he answered my prayer. I am a witness that God hears, and he answers.

Father God, you said if we don't have, then we should ask. I ask you for clarity, new visions, peace, good health, divine order, and great destiny helpers. As I travel this road of life, I realize each day that I need you more and more. I ask you to give me new opportunities with open doors of blessings. I will continuously seek your face because I know you have new mercies, new grace, and favor for me each day. Thank you for your unwavering commitment to bless me. I will continue to knock at the blessing door because it is there, and I will find you. Have your way in my life Father, have thine own way. Thank you for the many blessings. Amen.

GOOD SEED

Therefore, all things whatsoever ye would that men should do to you, do ye
even so to them: for this is the law and the prophets.
Matthew 7:12 (KJV)

Remember: you sow a bad seed, you reap a bad one; but if you sow a good seed, you reap a good one. Treat others the way you would like to be treated. Don't spread hateful lies about people to make them look bad and to make yourself look good. That is not the will of God. Thou shall not lie. We all should strive to be in right standing with God. We do not bow to strife, envy, back-biting, backstabbing, jealousy and wrongdoing. Instead, we lift up the name of Jesus in all that we do. We stand on the promises of God because his word is true. God is faithful in his love for us. We give honor and praise to the creator of the universe. We serve a worthy God, and he deserves a worthy praise. We bless the name of the Lord.

Lord God, I expect to receive good. Therefore, I will treat my fellowman with respect and honor. You said to feed those who are hungry, clothe those who are naked, and visit those in prison. You have given me your commandments so that I will know how to treat others. Father, I will keep your commandments and I will do unto others as I would have them do to me. I will greet my sisters and brothers with love and not hate. I will be kind to them. Thank you, Father, for giving me a heart of love. Love is kind and not puffed up. I will walk in humility as I seek to do your will here in the earth realm. I draw near to you Father. Thank you for your loving kindness. Amen.

THE MOUTH SPEAKS

Oh, generation of vipers, how can ye, being evil, speak good things? For out of the abundance of the heart the mouth speaks.
Matthew 12:34 (KJV)

Listen: be careful about what you say. Actually, you should think before you speak. Words are powerful and therefore can be upsetting if used in a harmful context. They can also be deadly. As a young girl, I was told a story about some adults playing a friendly game of cards. One of the men thought the other was cheating, so he confronted him about it. It was what he said that mattered. He called the man a horrible name. The other man asked him not to call him that again. But the man insisted on degrading the man as he described how he was cheating in the card game. The accused cheater pulled out a gun and killed the man. This man lost his life over a few negative words. These negative words were in his heart, and he spoke them causing him to be killed instantly. Please think before you speak. You just can't say everything that comes to your mind. Ponder on it.

Lord God, I bind up every evil thing that tries to attack my body, my speech, and my mind. Let nothing but purity come from my heart. Let your words flow from my tongue. I will bless thee oh Lord. Father, I vow to do good and not evil. Keep my heart clean so that I may walk worthy of the calling you have placed on my life. I honor you with my life and I repent of every foul spirit that has kept me captive. You are my savior and my lifeline. Let the words of my mouth and the meditation of my heart be acceptable in thy sight oh lord my strength and my redeemer. Keep me in your loving arms so I may do your will. Amen.

IN THE MIDST

For where two or three are gathered in my name,
there am I in the midst of them.
Matthew 18:20 (KJV)

Jesus is always present when you are in agreement. It's prayer time! Being together for agreement doesn't mean you have to always be together in a physical manner. There is no distance in the power of prayer because God is everywhere. One of my church members and I attended a women's conference in a nearby county. After the worship service and a prayer walk, we were instructed to go to the family center for lunch and a round table discussion. There, a panel gave testimonies of their encounters with God. One lady said she received a statement from her credit card company billing her for something she had not purchased. She called and they kept putting her on hold giving her no answer. So, she contacted her prayer partner and told her what was happening because this was a very large amount charged to her account. She needed someone to agree with her that the company would take this false charge off her account. They kept her on the phone with one excuse after another. But she and her prayer partner kept praying. Finally, after two hours the company told her that all the false charges had been removed. God is in the midst.

Lord God, you said that "whatever I bind on earth would be bound in heaven and whatever I loose on earth would be loosed in heaven." I bind the stronghold that tries to come against me. I loose godly power. I thank you God that we can come together in your name and make our petitions known to you. Thank you for hearing our prayer and for answering our prayer. Amen.

YOU SHALL LOVE

Jesus said unto him, thou shalt love the Lord thy God with all thy heart,
and with all thy soul, and with all thy mind. This is the first and great
commandment. And the second is like unto it,
thou shalt love thy neighbor as thyself.
Matthew 22:37-39 (KJV)

Loving the Lord and loving your neighbor is first and foremost. Your neighbor is everyone you encounter. There was a meeting that included praying for those that desired prayer. Some skeptics attended the meeting and decided they would make up several sicknesses and tell the preacher they needed prayer. What they didn't know was that the preacher had a strong prophetic anointing. When it was their turn to ask for prayer, the preacher immediately called them out and told them what the Lord had shown him. Because they wanted to trick the man of God with a dishonest declaration of sickness, the Lord said these sicknesses would actually come upon them if they didn't repent. They cried out to God and instantaneously became believers of the Lord Jesus Christ. We don't play with God. We love him and we love his people, who are our neighbors.

Lord God, I will trust and obey you. Make me sensitive to your holy word. Cause my coming in and my going out to be blessed. I shall forever praise you, Lord God. I will be my brother's keeper. My neighbors will be blessed by my presence. I am mantled to be a blessing. Use me for your glory Lord God. I take authority over every evil thing, and I cast it into utter darkness. Thank you for being my first love. Amen.

WATCH AND PRAY

Watch and pray, that ye enter not into temptation:
the spirit indeed is willing, but the flesh is weak.
Matthew 26:41 (KJV)

Keep praying and guard your surroundings. Be in prayer constantly so that your spiritual antenna is sharp enough to detect any type of evil lurking around. The enemy likes to disguise himself so that he can generate deception among God's people. He comes in all different sizes, shapes, color, assignments, and positions. A hate group once held a rally in a nearby section of the county. The group tried to intimidate the rural residents by telling them that they were secretly everywhere in the county. They noted that they were in the school system, law enforcement, medical offices, legal system, and rescue recovery. They were unidentifiable that day, but they wanted everyone to know that they could see the people, but the people couldn't see them. Keep a diligent prayer life.

Heavenly Father, I will obey you. I will keep your commandments. I will follow after you. I will break all soul ties that are corrupt and of no effect. Deliver me from the hands of the enemy. Lead me into all truth. Keep me in a safe place. Your word shall forever be in my mouth and my heart so that I will not sin against you. Strengthen my body and my mind. Cause me to have clean thoughts. Give me the anointing to be able to know the times and seasons. I bind every fleshy tendency that tries to creep into my life. I declare that I am anointed and appointed by you Father. From this day forward I will walk worthy of your love. Thank you for strengthening me. Amen.

HAVE WHAT YOU SAY

For verily I say unto you, that whosoever shall say unto this mountain,
be thou removed, and be thou cast into the sea; and shall not doubt in his heart,
but shall believe that those things which he saith shall come to pass,
he shall have whatsoever he saith.
Mark 11:23 (KJV)

Trust the Lord when you pray, and you shall have what you say. Ask according to God's will, trust his unlimited power, believe his word to be true, and don't allow doubt to creep in, and you shall have what you say. My son did not have the chickenpox when he was a young child, but he had it when he was a teenager. People asked if I had it as a child, and I did not. So, they told me that I was going to get it from him. I immediately said, "No I will not get it from him." They kept trying to put that disease on me, but I kept denying it. I can remember walking through the house declaring and decreeing that I would not get the chickenpox. And it was established that I didn't get it.

Lord God, my faith is strong because I believe your word. You are the one and only true living God. If you tell me to speak to the enemy that is attacking my life or the life of a loved one, I will do so. I will take authority over that demonic spirit and cast it down throwing it into the sea. There will be no doubt in my heart because I believe your word is true. You told me to do this, and the blessing will be mine. I speak to every mountain of evil that tries to invade my life and I command it to stop! Thank you, Lord God, for building my faith and giving me the authority to have what I say. I bless your holy name. Amen.

STRONG FAITH

And he said unto her, Daughter, be of good comfort:
thy faith hath made thee whole; go in peace.
Luke 8:48 (KJV)

Wouldn't you love to be healed because of your strong faith? Daughter, why do you seek attention from every other source except the one who loves you beyond measure? Why do you think you will find comfort in the company of a stranger? Don't wait until there is an issue (sickness, hurt, shame) in life to seek God; seek him now! You need God on speed dial – call him up! As a Christian, I was told shortly after the birth of my son that I had a rare heart issue. At the time, there was no known medical cure for such condition. I continued my persistent journey as a Christian, giving this ailment to the Lord. Years later during my annual check-up, it was noted that there was no issue with my heart. My trust and confidence in God made me whole.

Lord God, I am healed by your stripes. I declare that no weapon formed against me shall prosper. I call forth ministering angels to battle on my behalf. I reject pain, sick and disease. Sickness has no place in my life. I bind every form of witchcraft that seeks to take me out. My body is whole. My mind is sound. I am covered by the blood of Jesus. I have victory over death and the grave. Jesus Christ has paid the price at Calvary for me. I do not accept sickness and disease. Sickness and disease must flee from my body. I am the righteousness of God. You told me I could lay hands on the sick and they would recover. I operate in your power and authority. I lay hands on my body and declare healing. Thank you for the anointing of grace. Amen.

THE BEGINNING

In the beginning was the Word, and the Word was with God,
and the Word was God.
John 1:1 (KJV)

We all need the word of God. It is life for our very existence. This passage tells us of the power of God and how eternal he is. It tells us he was and he is. So, there is no getting around him or trying to run and hide from him. He is the God of all creation. My mother told us that her older brother said that God called him to preach. Uncle was a very smart man, I am told, but did not want to be in the pulpit. Mother said he constantly ran from his spiritual assignment, instead living by the world's standard. This was a dangerous lifestyle, and it ultimately got him into trouble. He died on his 40th birthday. God does not beg us or force us to love him. He gives us freewill. It is our choice to serve him or serve the world. Our choices have consequences.

Father God, I receive you as my Lord and Savior. I honor you as the Most High Priest. I understand that as I read your word, I am talking to you because you are the word. I love your teachings. I love how you guide me by giving me insight and revelation knowledge. Your word is true, your word is you and I reverence you through the word. Oh, how powerful and mighty you are. You spoke this world into existence. Father, this tells me how powerful and how important my words are here in the earth. I shall speak peace, joy, happiness, prosperity, good health, and good wealth. My mouth will be filled with your words. Miracles, signs, and wonders shall follow as I give thanks unto you. I am forever grateful for your guidance. Amen.

NO GREATER LOVE

For God so loved the world, that he gave his only begotten Son, that whosoever believeth in him should not perish, but have everlasting life.
John 3:16 (KJV)

There is no greater love than that of our heavenly Father. Sometimes things can happen in life that can really get our attention. It's a wake-up call that we must answer. God loves us so much that he gives us a second chance. The enemy will aim to take us out, but God says "no, that is my child." He loves us beyond our faults. When my son had to have a very serious surgery, he got a cross with tear drops tattooed on his back. John 3:16 was written at the bottom of the cross. This was an awakening for him because he realized that God didn't have to spare his life, but he did. He truly came to the very knowledge of God's unlimited and timely love for him. God will not force us, but he will guide us. He will guide us through our darkness hour.

Father God, I bless your holy name. You are the God above all gods. You gave us your only son so that we could live in right standing with you. You gave us your best gift and for that I say thank you Father. You are magnificent. I am in awe of you. You are so good to us, and we don't deserve it. You have looked beyond our faults and see after our needs. This is underserved kindness. I am so thankful. You are God the Father, God the Son, and God the Holy Spirit. I worship you in spirit and in truth. I adore you, Father. There is none other like you. I give you all the honor and all the praise. Everlasting life is my portion. Hallelujah to God! Amen.

WHAT'S IN YOUR HEART

He that believeth on me, as the scripture hath said,
out of his belly shall flow rivers of living water.
John 7:38 (KJV)

What's in your heart? Is it the word of God? If so, then it will flow to others giving them encouragement, peace, joy, and love. When your heart is full of the word of God, your speech is laced with a sweet acceptable flavor. People will enjoy being around you. They know you will exalt God at all times. When they need to be inspired or reassured, they will give you a call. They know the word of God is flowing through you. They recognize your deep love for Father God. They know that you are an intercessor and from your innermost being you will allow God to have his way. Speak Lord, speak.

Father God, I keep your word in my heart so that I will not sin against you. You word is life to me. I ingest your word daily so that I may walk worthy of my calling. I draw near to your so that you will draw near to me. I need you every day in my life. Speak to my heart and give me ears to hear what thus saith the Lord God. Allow your word to penetrate my heart so that from it your words will flow. Open my eyes so that I may see what you see. Cause me to be a good steward and a blessing to others. I will speak of your greatness. I will testify of your goodness. My God, you are excellent. I exalt thee, oh Lord, and I lift up your name in all the earth. If it had not been for the Lord on my side, where would I be? Thank you, Father for your unwavering love for me. I am yours. Use me for your glory. Amen.

FREE INDEED

If the Son therefore shall make you free, ye shall be free indeed.
John 8:36 (KJV)

Jesus has made us free! He has paid the price at Calvary. It does not matter what you have done, if you repent and give your life to Jesus, he will forgive you and set you free. One Sunday, a young lady visited our church. She was apparently in the back crying profusely. The usher came to me ask if I would go in the foyer and speak to her. She was already surrounded by several other prayer warriors. She thought that she had done something so horrible that God would not forgive her. We prayed with her and then I told her that no matter what she had done, God still loved her and would forgive her. She looked at me in amazement and asked, "No matter what?" I assured her that no sin was too big for God. Be still and know that he is God. He is the almighty God.

Lord God, thank you for setting me free from condemnation, rejection, deception, depression, distractions, intimidation, manipulation, poverty, not having enough, denial, delay, hindering spirits, seducing spirits, lying spirits, sickness and disease, witchcraft, hatred, envy, jealousy, pre-mature death, suicide, murder, corruption, greed, back stabbing, demonic attacks, controlling spirits, haughtiness, high-mindedness, ungodly soul ties, and every demonic spirit that seeks to attach itself to me. I will not be bound by any demonic force. I plead the blood of Jesus over all my situations, circumstances, family, friends, my government, all schools, all churches, the medical field, the entertainment field, business, and all systems. Thank you, God for making us free to serve you. Amen.

ABUNDANT LIFE

The thief cometh not, but for to steal, and to kill, and to destroy: I am come
that they might have life, and that they might have it more abundantly.
John 10:10 (KJV)

God has given you an abundant life, so don't let the enemy take it away!
God wants you to have abundance in love, peace, happiness, joy, good
health, wealth, family matters, business transactions, education, courage,
strength, etc. He wants you to have abundance in wisdom, understanding,
and revelation knowledge. God wants you to live the good life. God has
given us all things that pertain to life and godliness. He wants the very best
for us. He has given us free will to choose the road we take. If we choose
the ungodly road and get into trouble, allowing the enemy to rob us of the
good life, we cannot blame God.

---

*Lord God, you are my shield, my refuge my fortress and in you I hide myself. I give
my life to you, and I ask you to use me for your glory. It is not my will to be done here
on the earth, but it is your will that must be done. When the enemy seeks to devour
me, hide me in the cleft of the rock. Keep me in your secret place. I know the enemy
is like a thief that comes in the night to steal, kill, and destroy; but I know you have
come to give me that abundant life. Thank you, God, for abundance, for angelic
assistance, and for satisfying me with long life. When I call upon you, I know you
will answer. You are a gracious God. I love you, Lord God. I am determined to do
your will. This is your servant's prayer. Amen.*

LIFTED UP

And I, if I be lifted up from the earth, will draw all men unto me.
John 12:32 (KJV)

Are you lifting up the name of Jesus? He was lifted up on the cross for all of us. He paid the ultimate price for our freedom. Every opportunity we get, we should boast of his goodness. As we lift up his wonderful name, others should be drawn to him through us. Being a witness for Christ is our job. People shouldn't have to pump and probe us to see if we are a Christian. This should be evident the moment they meet us. Christ, the hope of glory, should shine brightly through us, causing men and women to want to know more about him. It's witnessing time. Get out into the hedges, highways, and byways and proclaim that Jesus is Lord. Let them know that he is Lord over all.

Heavenly Father, your son, Jesus Christ gave his life for me. I will forever be grateful for such love. The son of man was lifted up on the cross, beaten, died, rose on the third day with all power in his hands, ascended back to heaven and now is sitting at the right hand of the Father. All of this just so that I may have an abundant life. I surrender my life to you Heavenly Father. I will lift up the name of Jesus. I will celebrate your goodness. I will hide your word in my heart. Father, let my light shine so that people will see your righteousness through me. I am an ambassador of Jesus Christ. I will respect and obey you because this is the beginning of wisdom. I will worship you with fear and trembling. I owe my life to you. Thank you for being upright and worthy. I love you. Amen.

ABIDE FOREVER

And I will pray the Father, and he shall give you another Comforter,
that he may abide with you forever.
John 14:16 (KJV)

Did you know that Jesus is with you all the time? How cool is that! God's word tells us that if we make our bed in hell, he is with us. In other words, it does not matter how deep you fall into sin, you can always cry out to Jesus, and he will hear you. This is absolutely wonderful news. God has given of himself in the form of the Holy Spirit to be with us at all times. It is similar to you teaching your children right from wrong. When they are away from you and find themselves in the middle of mischief, they will hear your voice and the words you spoke to them. The Holy Spirit is with us to guide and direct us into all truths.

Father God, thank you for sending me the comforter (Holy Spirit) to always be with me, to help me, and to guide me. Father, I thank you for your son, Jesus Christ who gave his life for me. Father, you are so generous with your love. I have failed you many times. I have not kept your word, yet you still provided for me. As I abide in your word, you cause me to be an overcomer. I am just amazed at your commitment to me. You are a loving daddy with whom I am well pleased. I can never repay you for all your kindness, compassion, and thoughtfulness you've shown me. When I consider your greatness, I am in awe of you. Holy Spirit, speak to my heart so that I will be in tune with the step of the Father. I love you God because you have never left me even when I didn't know you, you were there by my side. You are so praiseworthy. I love you God. Amen.

ASK WHAT YE WILL

If ye abide in me, and my words abide in you,
ye shall ask what ye will, and it shall be done unto you.
John 15:7 (KJV)

Being a good child of the King, we get good gifts! This is the good life for kingdom citizens. God wants to shower us with many blessings. He desires an abundant life for his children. He has given us the blueprint – remain in him by studying his word so that he remains in us. We hide his word in our hearts so that sin will not creep into our emotions. We allow his word to be alive in us so that the Holy Spirit will speak to us. We delight in him and keep his commandments. We draw near to him because he is within us. Developing a personal relationship with Father God will cause angels to war on our behalf and we will operate in the overflow of his many blessings. Unite with God.

Heavenly Father, you said if I stay connected to you and your word, that what I ask for you will provide. If I had ten thousand tongues, I could not thank you enough for being so gracious to me. You are a loving Father, and I owe my life to you. I honor you in all I do. I will obey your teachings. I find comfort in knowing that I have such a loving daddy. You have blessed me and my bloodline. And for that, I say thank you. If it had not been for you Father, I don't know where I would be. When the enemy tried to snuff me out, you made him stand back and behave. I am a living testimony of your love for mankind. I will praise you in the morning, noon day and at night. Your praises will continually be in my mouth. Thank you, Father. Amen.

BELIEVE ON THE LORD

And they said, believe on the Lord Jesus Christ,
and thou shalt be saved, and thy house.
Acts 16:31 (KJV)

Following the teachings of the Lord Jesus Christ, your household will be saved – that's good news! When you accept the Lord Jesus Christ as your personal savior and dedicate yourself to him, you will witness to everyone in your household. As a matter of fact, you will probably witness to everyone in your entire family. This is such a beautiful thing to allow the spirit of God to flow through you as you are being a witness for the kingdom. This is living the life that God meant for us – the spirit-filled life. A life that honors him. Honoring him in all areas. When we do business, we do it God's way.

Heavenly Father, you said to believe in your son, the Lord Jesus Christ, and salvation will not only be my portion, but it will be for my entire household. What a blessing this is to me! My faith is set in you. Jesus Christ is Lord over my life. I am purposed to follow the word of the Lord all of my days. Thank you, Father for giving me godly counsel through Jesus Christ. Thank you for giving me ears to hear what thus saith the Lord. Thank you for eyes to see so that I may know the changing of the times and seasons. For I know the plans that you have for me Father, plans to cause me to do good and not evil. You will show me great and mighty things that I can only receive from you. Thank you for provision and insight. I receive this in Jesus' name. Amen.

ALL THINGS

And we know that all things work together for good to them that love God,
to them who are the called according to his purpose.
Romans 8:28 (KJV)

No matter what the situation is, God is still at work! I love this! When I can't trace him or track him, he is still working on my behalf. This is totally awesome. There have been times when I wanted to cry out and say, "God where are you?" I was in my valley experience wondering if I would ever get out. Needless to say, God was giving me a testimony at that time. We cannot expect God to be like a puppet. He is very strategic and progressive. He has a plan, and he will complete it step by step. God is always working behind the scenes because he knows the end from the beginning. It is comforting to know that whatever situation I find myself in, God can turn it around for my good.

Lord God, you chose me before I was formed in my mother's womb. You knew me and you had good thoughts and a good course for my life. Your divine destiny has always been my portion. However, sometimes I have strayed away from the original plan. Forgive me God. I have ignored your hand on my life and decided to do my own thing. But you are so loving, you caused everything to work for my good...even the not-so-good. You turned the bad incidents around to work in my favor. You are a just God. Thank you for always being at work on my behalf. You turn my midnight (dark times) into daylight. You cause the sun to shine (in my life) on a cloudy day. Thank you for choosing me as your servant. I will forever be faithful to you. You are magnificent in all your ways. I love you God. Amen.

CONFESSION

That if thou shalt confess with thy mouth the Lord Jesus, and shalt believe in thine heart that God hath raised him from the dead, thou shalt be saved.
Romans 10:9 (KJV)

It's just that simple – so be a witness! There are so many opportunities to witness to others. Sometimes we shy away and miss our chance. At other times, our very presence can be a witness because when people see your godly lifestyle, they become hungry for the same. They may not tell you, but you are the reason they are a Christian today. Years ago, one of my nephews came by my house asking for money. I perceived he was up to no good, so I asked if I could lead him into the prayer of salvation. He agreed, only if he wanted the money, but he still agreed. He repeated the prayer after me. Several months later he passed away. My heart was overwhelmed, but I'm so glad he prayed with me that day. Don't let an opportunity pass you by.

Heavenly Father, I confess with my mouth that Jesus is Lord and that you raised him from the dead. Thank you for salvation. Thank you for saving me from a burning hell. I acknowledge my sinful acts and I ask you for forgiveness Father. Wash me and clean me up. Make me new again so that I may serve you in spirit and in truth. Thank you, Father for your son, Jesus who gave his life for me. Thank you for the comforter, the Holy Spirit that lives in me, guides me, and instructs me. I operate under the grace of the Holy Spirit. My sins are forgiven. You are a forgiving God. Your mercy endures forever. I am yours Father. Use me for your glory. Amen.

REASONABLE SERVICE

I beseech you brethren, by the mercies of God, that ye present your bodies a living sacrifice, holy, acceptable unto God, which is your reasonable service.
Romans 12:1 (KJV)

A sanctified body is a consecrated body unto the work of the Lord. You have a made-up mind to follow the things of God and not the world. You will not straddle the fence and you will not be lukewarm. Some people come to church, and actually work in the church, but at other times they are secret street walkers. They are involved with so many people of the world that they become confused. They come into the church with the street mentality trying to use and misuse the Christians. This usually does not end well. God is not to be played with.

Lord God, I give you my body as a living sacrifice to use as a vessel here in the earth realm. I give you my mind so that your thoughts become my thoughts. I give you my ears so that I may hear what you are saying to the universal church. I give you my eyes so that I may see all the blind spots and trickery the enemy has plotted. I give you my hands so that I may receive the gift of healing to be a blessing to those that are battling sickness and disease. I give you my feet so that I may go into the hedges and highways to declare your name is great and you are greatly to be praised. I give you my voice so that I may speak of your good works and tell men and women everywhere I go that you are the savior of the world. Cleanse me Lord God so that I may do your will. This is your servant's prayer. Amen.

BROTHERLY LOVE

Be kindly affectioned one to another with brotherly love;
in honour preferring one another.
Romans 12:10 (KJV)

Being kind to others will cost you nothing! I love a career where I get to help people. Not only do I help them, but I gain a friend. It is so rewarding and fulfilling to be an extension of Christ while on the job. This is what I call a "happy job" because I get to do the work assigned to me by my immediate supervisor and by my Lord and Savior. There is plenty to do because there are so many people who are in need, hurting, without family, and so alone. We can share the love of Jesus Christ with them by simply being kind and helpful. The songster wrote: "What the World Needs Now is Love." I totally agree because there is definitely enough hate going around in the world. Let us love.

Heavenly Father, create in me a clean heart and give me your holy spirit to guide and teach me so that I will have love for my sisters and brothers in Christ. Cause me to operate in integrity and decency, respecting those I come in contact with. I will treat my fellowman with an upright spirit. Father, you said in your word to love thy neighbor as thyself. Help me to be a good neighbor and a good witness for you. I will not gossip about others, but instead, lift them up in prayer. I will read your word and bring it back to you as I pray because your word will not return to you void. It will accomplish what it has said because you are a faithful God. Thank you for always being with me, as I walk this road called life. All praises are given to you. Amen.

HOLINESS

For the believing wife brings holiness to her marriage, and the believing husband brings holiness to his marriage.
Otherwise, your children would not be holy, but now they are holy.
1 Corinthians 7:14 (NLT)

My family is saved and consecrated to the things of God! Maybe the reason it is called holy matrimony is due to fact that the ceremony being performed is a holy thing between two believers. Marriage should be sacred and holy; however, in these days, one cannot say that this is always the case. We should love our spouse as Christ loves the church. It is a beautiful thing when two believers come together in marriage. Their children will be brought up in the way of the Lord. The entire household will serve God. What a great legacy to leave within the family. The blessings of the Lord will be from generation to generation.

Father God, cause me to be a good parent. To set a good example for my children. To walk worthy of the calling you have placed on my life. Let my children rise up and call me blessed. Let them always respect me as a parent. Do not let my living be in vain, but cause it to be a great testimony to the goodness of your love. I will obey you at all times. Your praises shall continually be in mouth. Your word tells me that you are holy so therefore I shall be holy. Thank you for a life of holiness. Thank you for your son, Jesus Christ, who came to give me an abundant life, a life filled with the Holy Spirit. You are a Holy God and I bow down before you; I adore you, I worship you, and I love you. Thank you, God, that my entire household is saved. Amen.

GOD OF PEACE

For God is not a God of disorder but of peace,
as in all meetings of God's holy people.
1 Corinthians 14:33 (NLT)

Conduct yourselves in a godly manner, lest you be caught up in confusion. Everyone has an opinion, and they feel their opinion is correct. But that is exactly what it is: an opinion. An opinion is a view of something without any facts or concrete knowledge. God wants us to live, work, and fellowship in peace. God is about peace and order. With much prayer and making our petition known, God will give us peace that surpasses all understanding. The worries of the world will not consume us with fear and doubt because we know who holds tomorrow.

Lord God, you are a God of order. You are a God of peace. Let us conduct ourselves decently and in order at all times. Lord God, I do not want to be a person that is always out of order. Nor do I want to be a person that is constantly calling attention to myself. I do not want to be a person that has to be the center of attention or a person that is always bragging and boasting about what I have done. Your word tells me that boasting is not a good thing unless I am boasting of your goodness. I do not bring notice to myself, but I bring notice to you, God. I will tell of your greatness; you made the heavens and the earth; you own the cattle on a thousand hills; you are the maker and creator of all perfect gifts. Whatever I have achieved or gain in this life, I owe it all to you. I will always acknowledge you as the leader of my life. I can do nothing without you. Lead me and guide me oh Lord. I relinquish my life to you. Use me for your glory. Amen.

DECENTLY AND IN ORDER

Let all things be done decently and in order.
1 Corinthians 14:40 (KJV)

Learn how to act according to the word of God. Many like to take matters into their own hands. We should seek God for direction in any type of situation. He knows all and sees all, so he won't be surprised by anything you ask. He said that we have not because we ask not. Bring it to Jesus, he can definitely handle it. Before stepping out on your own conclusion of the matter, consult with King Jesus. See what he has to say about the situation. Pray, read the word of God, and wait for him to either give you the answer directly or show you the way. He knows.

Father God, cause me to be polite and courteous in all my ways. Help me to walk upright and be watchful. Help me to always be in tune with the things that are going on around me so that I don't fall into harm's way. I will continuously seek your will for my life. I will act according to your word. I will not be unpleasant to others. I will treat my neighbor – which is everyone I come in contact with – as myself. I will show forth your love in the earth. I will be a supporter of the gospel of Jesus Christ. Your word Father God will I hid in my heart so that I will not sin against you. My desire is that when others see me, they will first see you in me. They will know that I am a child of the Most High God. And as I speak to others, your love for them will become evident and they will begin to seek after you. So many people need you God. Help me to be a good witness for you. I love you, Father God. Amen.

THE WORK OF THE LORD

Therefore, my beloved brethren, be ye steadfast, unmovable, always abounding
in the work of the Lord, forasmuch as ye know
that your labor is not in vain in the Lord.
1 Corinthians 15:58 (KJV)

Do that which is good – stand on the word. God will never lead you down a wrong path. Staying connected with God is the best thing one can do. The world has so much negativity to offer us, but we must remain diligent in the work of the Lord. We must pray for the gift of discerning of spirits so that we can tell the good from the evil. Doing our best and going above and beyond the call of duty is pleasing in the sight of God. Help others as well as pray for them. People need prayer but they also need tangible items, godly instructions, and directions. "Give a man a fish and you feed him for a day. Teach him to fish and you feed him for a lifetime." This is so true, noting that more needs to be done. Help can come in many different forms. Be a helper.

Father God, I need you every hour of every day. I will always stand firm on your word. I will not be shaken or deceived by the tricks of the enemy. I serve the eviction notice on the enemy. He must flee from me. He has no authority in my life. I bind, rebuke, and cancel every plan and strategy of the enemy. I know that victory is mine because your mercy and grace flows to me. The blood of Jesus protects me and covers me. Therefore, I will stand my ground and proclaim the goodness of the Lord. I will work while it is day; while I have strength in my body to do your will. I submit myself unto your authority Father God. I am your humble servant. Use me for your glory. Amen.

THERE IS LIBERTY

Now the Lord is that Spirit:
and where the Spirit of the Lord is, there is liberty.
II Corinthians 3:17 (KJV)

Freedom to love, serve and be a blessing to others is wonderful because that means we are not in any type of bondage. There is physical bondage and there is spiritual bondage. If one breaks the law and becomes a criminal, physical bondage may occur. But so many people are in spiritual bondage in their minds. They have encountered the wrong crowd that has filled their mind with false information leaving them confused. This has caused many to be afflicted with mental illnesses. Allowing the spirit of the Lord to be our guide, in life and in all things, will set us free from the schemes of the enemy. God wants to be our guiding light. He longs for us to draw near to him. The more we allow the spirit of the living God to rest, rule and abide within us, the more we will walk in the freedom he wants for us.

Lord God, I just want to be more and more like you each day. Wherever your Spirit is, there is freedom. Holy Spirit invade my life! There is nothing separating me from the love of God. I am delivered from bondage that torments by mind and body. I bind every unclean spirit of fear, rejection, depression, heaviness, worry, uncertainty, confusion, trauma, and past hurt. Thank you, God, for setting me free from sin that I knowingly committed and unknowingly committed. Lord God, I thank you that deliverance is my portion. I find peace in being connected to you. I shall wear the garment of praise. I give you honor and glory. Amen.

A NEW CREATURE

Therefore, if any man be in Christ, he is a new creature: old things are passed
away; behold, all things are become new.
II Corinthians 5:17 (KJV)

Looking through the eyes of Jesus Christ, we see new life! We are no longer that sinful creature indulging in naughtiness and mischief. We have received Jesus Christ as our Lord and Savior and now we are a new creature in Christ. We don't associate with the old crowd anymore, go to the old hangout, or do and say the things we used to. We have been cleansed by the blood of Jesus. We walk in the newness of Christ. We are a new creature with a new attitude. When God invades our life, we even look different. In church we used to sing, "I've been changed since Jesus came into my life. I look at my hands and they look new, look at my feet and they do too." God is doing a new thing.

Heavenly Father, thank you for son, Jesus Christ who bore my sins at Calvary. Thank you for the blood that was shed on my behalf. I can never repay you for giving me your best gift: Jesus Christ. I know that by receiving Jesus Christ into my life, I put the past behind me. I am now a new person in Jesus Christ. I have a new disposition, a new attitude, a new outlook on life. I receive all the gifts Jesus has for me. I will live in the Spirit, and I will walk in the Spirit. Thank you, Father, for the newness in my life. Cause me to connect with the right people. Order my steps. Be a lamp unto my feet and light unto my path. Lead me and guide me in a straight way. I want my work here on earth to be pleasing in your sight. I am a new person in Christ. Amen.

PRAYING THROUGH

For though we walk in the flesh, we do not war after the flesh.
II Corinthians 10:3 (KJV)

Praying through the problem and pulling down strongholds is what we do instead of fighting hand to hand. The flesh is weak, so naturally we sometimes would rather go toe to toe with the adversary. God did not command us to fight our way through every problem or situation. God fights our battles. Vengeance is his and he will repay the enemy. All we got to do is keep a very close relationship with God the Father and watch him take care of those difficult moments in our life. At times, our culture will dictate an atmosphere of revenge, but we've got to learn to take our troubles to the Lord and not to the streets. Violence will not solve the problem; it only causes it to escalate the more.

Father God, thank you for your Holy Spirit that causes me to walk in a godly manner and not create an atmosphere of trouble and pain. I live in the world, but I do not do worldly things that causes much confusion and animosity. You said in your word that you have come so that I may have life and have it more abundantly. I live in abundance of your love, grace, and mercy. I pull down every stronghold of intimidation and manipulation. I bind, rebuke, and cast down every seducing spirit, lying spirit, and familiar spirit. Whom the son sets free is free indeed. I replace every curse of the enemy with a blessing. I counterattack the enemy with the power of the Holy Spirit. I send the enemy back to the pit of hell and I close the door. I declare and decree this in Jesus' name. Amen.

GRACE TO ENDURE

Each time he said, my grace is all you need. My power works best in weakness.
So now I am glad to boost about my weaknesses,
so that the power of Christ can work through me.
II Corinthians 12:9 (NLT)

Grace to endure – for Christ is the perfect one! God's strength is made perfect in our weakness. No one can take the credit for what has been done because it is evident that it is a God thing. When the doctor says there is nothing else, he can do and the patient recovers, you know that it is the hand of God. We had a family member that was very ill years ago. As a matter of fact, she was on life support and her organs were shutting down. The doctor called the family in to see her one last time before they disconnected the life support. They took her off it, yet she is still living today. The power of God rested upon her and raised her up. His grace is sufficient for all of us. What a mighty God!

Heavenly Father, you are all I need. You will lead and guide me to safe places and to the right people at the right time. I may not know which way to turn or which way to go, but you know all things. When I fall into the wrong company, your grace is sufficient to rescue me. When I have relapsed into old habits and old friends your grace picks me up, washes me and set me on a straight path. You are the God of breakthrough. When I fall into diverse temptations, you cause me to breakthrough without any residue. I will lift up the name of Jesus who works through me and in me to be victorious. I am in full agreement with Jesus Christ who paid the price at Calvary. There is no greater love. Amen.

I AM CRUCIFIED

I am crucified with Christ: nevertheless I live; yet not I, but Christ liveth in me:
and the life which I now live in the flesh I live by the faith of the Son of God,
who loved me, and gave himself for me.
Galatians 2:20 (KJV)

Dying to self and living a life that's pleasing to God is a daily deal. We should practice daily dying to sinful thoughts and actions. Jesus Christ went to the cross so that I may have a life free from sin. The least I can do is to honor what he did. I live in this body that I have surrendered to him and I now have the mind of Christ because I live by his faith in me. He has given me all of him, and now I give him all of me. I choose to die to sin. This is one of my favorite scriptures because it exemplifies the powerful love God has for all of us. To give his only begotten son so that we might have eternal life. People say they love you, but God really shows you that he loves you.

Father, I have died to sin because Jesus Christ took my sin away on the cross at Calvary. Yet, I still live! It is Jesus Christ in me that causes me to live a life of holiness. This fleshly body I am in lives through the faith of the Son of God who loved me so much that he gave his life for me. This is astonishing! This is really true love. There is no greater love than that of a man who lays down his life for a friend. Father, I can hardly comprehend that someone could love me this much. I will embrace this love of God the Father, God the Son and God the Holy Spirit has for me. I will forever express my gratitude for such enormous love. I will die to selfish deeds and selfish tendencies daily. This profound love is overwhelmingly the work of grace. Thank you, Father, for a love that surpasses all understanding. You are magnificent, superb, marvelous and oh so glorious. You deserve all the praise. Thank you for loving me. Amen.

IN THE SPIRIT

If we live in the Spirit, let us also walk in the Spirit.
Galatians 5:25 (KJV)

Living a spirit-filled life is the life of the believer. The believer has personal integrity, godly character, and honorable courage. Believers possess honesty, and they do things decently and in order. They have good moral standards, and their conduct is empowered by the Holy Spirit. They follow the golden rule – treat others as you would have them treat you. The spirit-filled believers do not go around starting confusion, discord, and deception. They do not operate in intimidation and manipulation. You cannot corrupt them because of their walk with Jesus. They have been empowered by Jesus the Christ.

Father God, I thank you for your Holy Spirit that rules and reigns in my life. I have not always deserved your Spirit dwelling in me, but I thank you for giving me the Comforter. At times, I have been a bad child before a good daddy. I repent of all sins. I will bind false witnesses that try to come against me. I give my life to you so that I will walk in the Spirit. This is a new season in my life. This is a new season for healing, good health, prosperity, favor, more grace, abundance, strength, and doors of great opportunity opening for me. I will be obedient to your will and to your way. I will consult you because you are the mighty counselor. I thank you for this new season and all that you have planned for me to accomplish. Your Spirit causes me to be happy, peaceful, patient, kind and full of faith. I will be a good steward in the body of Christ. This is your servant's prayer. Amen.

BE NOT DECEIVED

Be not deceived; God is not mocked: for whatsoever a man soweth, that shall he also reap.
Galatians 6:7 (KJV)

It's time to stop being a player – get real, people! You cannot trick God with your sorcery and witchcraft. He will not allow you to make fun of him and try to imitation him for profit.

Father God, I come before you with clean hands and a clean heart. I desire to do your will here in the earth. Not my will be done, but yours. I follow after you because I need you every day, in every situation, and in every area of my life. I will not take you for granted, but I will esteem you higher than any person or any event. A grand door of success opening is only because of you. A miracle in the midst of hard times is only because of you. You are above all because you made all and you know all. I will not run ahead of you, but I will seek your wisdom and guidance for my life. I will be like a farmer who plants a seed. I will water it. I will nurture it. When it grows, I will pull the weeds from around it. This will cause me to have a good harvest. As I give your word back to you in prayer, I will continue to stand on that word by confessing it and believing for a great outcome. You said your word will not return to you void, but it shall accomplish that which you please, and it shall prosper in the thing you sent it to. I declare that I shall reap goodness, peace, prosperity, favor, grace, and abundance. Thank you, Father for your word. Amen.

BE YE KIND

Let all bitterness, and wrath, and anger, and clamour, and evil speaking be put away from you, with all malice: And be ye kind one to another, tenderhearted, forgiving another, even as God for Christ's sake hath forgiven you.
Ephesians 4:31-32 (KJV)

Don't allow evil to rule your life because it will eventually destroy you. By speaking foul, worthless words, the door opens for the enemy to attack your life. We must realize that the enemy is just waiting for us to say or do the wrong thing. And when we do, his demons spring into action. Let's not put our sisters and brothers down with vulgar language. This is not being who God has created us to be. And if they speak abusive about you, let it go. Please don't retaliate with ugly words. Learn to forgive and turn these situations over to King Jesus. People will be people who operate from their own evil thought process. We cannot control how they feel about us. But we can pray for them.

Lord God, in your word you said, "vengeance is mine; I will repay" saith the Lord. That tells me that you will fight my battle. All I have to do is stand still and see the goodness of the Lord. I know you will turn the situation around and cause it to work for my good. All I have to do is put my trust in you. I will not grieve the Holy Spirit by allowing unjust, bad thoughts, jealously and envy to invade my heart. However, I will be kind, forgiving and just to all mankind because you forgave me of my sins. I will extend that same mercy and grace to my fellowman. Thank you for godly instructions and wisdom to function in a worldly atmosphere. You are the master teacher. Amen.

RECOGNIZE THE ENEMY

For we wrestle not against flesh and blood, but against principalities, against powers, against the rulers of the darkness of this world, against spiritual wickedness in high places.
Ephesians 6:12 (KJV)

Know the enemy when you encounter him because he may be clothed in disguise. Pray for the gift of discerning of spirits so that you will recognize that which is good and that which is evil. The wolf will always come dressed in sheep's clothing. Beware!

Heavenly Father, I thank you for revelation knowledge and insight to foresee the tricks of the devil. Thank you for opening the eyes of my understanding so that I know I am not at war with human beings. You said whatever I bind on earth you would bind in heaven. I bind the wolf that is dressed in sheep's clothing trying to come against me with evil trickery. I bind every spirit of deception, distraction, dishonesty, depression, disappointment, and discord. I bind every controlling spirit, every spirit of intimidation, manipulation, witchcraft, denial, delay, poverty, sickness, disease, jealousy, strife, hatred, trauma, and confusion. I bind all seducing spirits and lying spirits. I bind a high-minded spirit, trouble-making spirit, pre-mature death, suicide, gossip, past hurt, childhood trauma, human trafficking, rape, incest, molestation, drug abuse, alcohol addiction, and prostitution. I dismantle the kingdom of darkness, and I render it null and void. I take authority over my mind, body, family, government, all schools, all churches, my business, and my surroundings. I declare the blessing of the Lord upon all that concerns me. Thank you for the gift of discerning of spirits. Amen.

A GOOD WORK

Being confident of this very thing, that he which hath begun a good work in you will perform it until the day of Jesus Christ.
Philippians 1:6 (KJV)

We put our confidence in Jesus Christ and not in man. Because it is Christ who will complete that which concerns us. I am reminded of the time I was driving home from school at night. It was very, very foggy and I could hardly see beyond the front of the car. I called my husband and told him how scary it was driving down this dark, foggy lonesome road by myself. He told me that I was not alone. He said, "Your passenger, Jesus Christ, is in the car with you." Immediately, I looked over to the passenger side and there, I could imagine a figure that looked like the Son of God riding with me. My fear disappeared and I traveled the next 40 miles home in peace. My confidence was empowered.

Father God, forgive us for having doubt and anxiety when we start a project, an event, or some type of program. And even when we have been called to do the work of the Lord. Your word tells me that you have not given me the spirit of fear, but that of power, and of love and of a sound mind. Therefore, I put all my trust in you because you have given me your word that you will see it to the end. My part is to stay connected to you. I put you at the head of my life so that I won't go astray. You are the Lord of my life, and I will continue to give you praise for the wonderful things you have in store for me. I will trust you completely and lean not to my own understanding, but in all my ways I will acknowledge you to lead and guide me in the right direction. Thank you for your guidance in my life. Amen.

THE MIND OF CHRIST

Let this mind be in you, which was also in Christ Jesus.
Philippians 2:5 (KJV)

Praying daily that we have the mind and heart of Christ. If we are to live the abundant life, then we must walk in humility as Jesus did when he was on the earth. Because we have surrendered our lives to Christ does not give us the right to act as though we are better than anyone else. The Holy Spirit unites us and causes us to be concerned for our fellowman. God does not appreciate a high-minded spirit. He does not want us to be jealous or proud, but rather humble, considering others more importantly than ourselves. God is the potter, and we are the clay. We ask him to shape us and mold us into what he would have us to be. We want to represent Christ well in the earth.

Heavenly Father, I bow down before you. I reverence you in all areas of my life. Fill me with your Holy Spirit. Wash me and make me clean. I want to be more and more like you each day. I thank you for your Son, Jesus Christ, who gave himself for the redemption of my sins. He came in such humility to save a wretch like me. I can never repay you Father, but I will spend my days pursuing your magnificent love. You are excellent in all your ways. I am so grateful for your unwavering affection for mankind. I declare that I have the mind of Christ to do your will here in the earth. The joy of the Lord is my strength. I will exalt the Lord at all times, your praises shall continually be in my mouth. Take control of my mind. Use me for your glory. Amen.

FORGETTING THOSE THINGS

Brethren, I count not myself to have apprehended: but this one thing I do,
forgetting those things which are behind,
and reaching forth unto those things which are before.
Philippians 3:13 (KJV)

We cannot go forward if we are stuck in the past. There are so many people dealing with childhood trauma. This trauma has robbed them of a happy, good, and comfortable life, a life with God. We know that we have not arrived because God is still working on us. He is continually purging us. He will always take us from glory to glory. Being with God makes each day better and better. He is causing all things to work for our good. We all need a close relationship with our heavenly Father. He is God.

Lord God, I humble myself before you. I give you full access to my life. I do not think highly of myself. I bow down before you. I adore you. I lift you up in all areas of my life. I am forever grateful to you. I put the past behind me, and I look to the hills from whence cometh my help. I know all my help comes from you God. You made the heavens and the earth and everything in the earth. I exalt thee oh Lord. You are a father for the fatherless and a mother for the motherless. You took care of me when I was yet in sin. I owe you, my life. I know that you have great and mighty things in store for me. I am more than a conqueror. So, I will press toward mark for the prize of the high calling of God in Christ Jesus. I will run this race with grace. Heaven shall be my eternal home. Thank you for your grace. Amen.

BE CAREFUL FOR NOTHING

Be careful for nothing; but in everything by prayer and supplication with
thanksgiving let your requests be made known unto God.
Philippians 4:6 (KJV)

Don't worry about the issues of tomorrow, be thankful for this day. This
is the day that the Lord has made, we will rejoice and be glad in it. We
will not worry about tomorrow because we know who holds tomorrow.
Anxiety will strip us of our peace. Give your worries to the Lord because
he can take care of any situation. Be thankful for the "now" in your life.
Now faith is the substance of things hope for and the evidence of things not
seen. With a grateful heart make your petition known to God. Cast your
cares upon him. He is more than capable to deal with the dilemma. Trust
and obey him. He is God almighty.

---

*Heavenly Father, thank you for the garment of praise. I will not entertain heaviness
or worry. Instead, I will give you my burdens because you are the burden bearer and
heavy load carrier. I cast my cares upon you because you care for me. You knew me
before I was formed in my mother's womb, and you blessed me before I entered the
earth realm. I will praise your holy name. I will be steadfast and unmovable always
abounding in your love. I will be faithful in my walk with you. Father, I come to you
with my needs in one hand and my wants in the other. I am making my requests
known to you. Thank you for hearing my prayer and for answering my prayer. I
give you all the glory. This is your servant's prayer. Amen.*

ALL THINGS

I can do all things through Christ which strengthens me.
Philippians 4:13 (KJV)

When you feel weak, Christ will strengthen you to get the job done. Even if you have doubts about your ability to complete the task, Jesus Christ is there to strengthen you physically and mentally. If you feel that this is not your area of expertise, ask Jesus to help you. Talk to him, he is waiting to hear from you. When I worked a temp job that was not in my study area (accounting) I asked the Lord to help me understand the new accounting system. I told him I couldn't do it without him and that I needed him to guide me through the process. And he did. Make your requests known to him with a grateful heart.

Lord God, various times I have fallen into divers (different) temptations. Temptation to speak out of term, to eat too much, to love too hard, to give what I don't have, to speak ill of others, to judge others, to let my emotions go too far, to be offended, to abhor wrong feelings toward others, to dislike my surroundings, to think more highly than I should, to allow my mind to wander aimlessly, and to think bad thoughts. I know I have done wrong, so I ask for forgiveness. I ask you God, to strengthen me to face any challenges that I might have in life. Your love covers a multitude of sin, so I give myself to you to shield me, to protect me, to guide me, to correct me and to sustain me. Keep me in a safe place. Protect me from the wicked plots of the enemy. Create in me a clean heart and renew your Holy Spirit within me. I know that I can do all things as you strengthen me daily. Thank you for the gift of the Holy Spirit. Amen.

ALL YOUR NEEDS

But my God shall supply all your needs according to
his riches in glory by Christ Jesus.
Philippians 4:19 (KJV)

Allow the one who has all to give you all that you need. He is our supplier of good things. He gives liberally and abundantly. A lady went to the beauty salon to have her hair done for a special occasion. The stylist encouraged her to have some weave put in to make a really beautiful style. When the lady returned to have the weave removed, it took her hair out. She didn't even realize it until she passed the mirror going to the shampoo area. She was devastated! The stylist didn't even apologize. But God is so good. It took a while, but the lady's hair grew back longer than what she previously had. God does supply.

Father God, you are my provider, my Jehovah Jireh. Just as you provided for Abraham a ram in the thick of the wilderness to replace his son, I know you will provide for me. You are a God of wonders, signs, and miracles. I thank you for blessing me with the things I need and also giving me things that I want. You are wonderful. I cannot praise you enough because you have always been there for me. You have looked beyond my faults and seen my needs. I have not always done that which is pleasing in you sight, but you still loved me. You have taken care of me despite my wrong doings. Your love for me goes beyond anything I have ever seen. Man sees the outer appearance, but Father you see my heart. Father, I give you all of me. Glory be God the Father, God the Son, and God the Holy Spirit. Amen.

WALK WORTHY

That ye might walk worthy of the Lord unto all pleasing, being fruitful in every good work, and increasing in the knowledge of God.
Colossians 1:10 (KJV)

Be obedient to the call on your life so you will bear much fruit. God has a plan and a purpose for each of us. He desires for us is to be healthy, wealthy, and wise. God gives us spiritual wisdom and insight of the task he set before us. When we develop a close relationship with our heavenly Father, he will anoint us with revelation knowledge causing us to have an admirable character that reflects who he is. We will operate in a manner that is worthy of the God that we serve. Others will know that the hand of the Lord is upon us because we have good moral integrity. God loves us.

Heavenly Father, cause me to live a life that is suitable and pleasing to you. You have delivered me from darkness into your marvelous light. You have snatched me from the jaws of the enemy. You have planted my feet on solid ground. You have given me a safe place. You have extended your victorious right hand to me. I shall forever be grateful for your love and kindness. Your words shall always be in my mouth, and I will meditate day and night to observe all that you have for me. Thank you for making my way prosperous and successful. I know that you want the best for me. Fill me with your knowledge, wisdom and understanding so that I may be a blessing to others. Thank you for your marvelous acts of kindness. I love you, Father. Amen

DO ALL IN HIS NAME

And whatsoever ye do in word or deed, do all in the name of the Lord Jesus,
giving thanks to God and the Father by him.
Colossians 3:17 (KJV)

Working in love and not in selfishness pleases Father God. Don't let your living be in vain, empty, useless, or pointless. Let your speech be that of encouragement because the word of God dwells in you. If you do a favor for someone, don't expect a favor back from that person. We speak life into all situations, and we help others because we have the love of Jesus in our hearts. No matter what you do, do it in the name of the Lord Jesus.

Lord God, you are so mighty! You are awesome! There is none like you in all the earth. I declare that the words of my mouth and the mediation of my heart be acceptable in your sight. I will intercede on behalf of my sisters and brothers in Christ. I will not speak negative of others. Negativity has no place in the kingdom of God. My deeds will be pure. I will not lend a helping hand just to see what I can get back in return. Your mercy flows to me despite my faults. I declare that I am the head and not the tail, above and not beneath, the lender and never the borrower. I am blessed coming in and blessed going out. I operate in the overflow of God. God's favor follows me. He gives me power to get wealth. Therefore, Lord God, my mouth will be filled with praises unto you. I am thankful that I am a conduit of blessings. I am obedient to your will and to your way of doing things. Use me for your glory. Amen.

YOUR SPEECH

Let your speech be always with grace, seasoned with salt,
that ye may know how ye ought to answer every man.
Colossians 4:6 (KJV)

Act like you know that you are a child of God. Represent well. Don't go to church on Sunday just to be a totally different person on Monday. This is what I call a bad witness. People get confused at your behavior, then they get discouraged and ultimately decide to not give their life to Jesus because they think all believers act like that. Your actions and speech should be gracious and pleasant. People should enjoy being in your presence. You should give them such a hunger and thirst for Christ each time you meet them. They should admire you from afar. They should strive to be more like you. Behave yourself.

Father God, guide my tongue. For I know that it can be wicked. It can and will defile the whole body. Teach me your ways so that I don't mistreat others. I will rejoice in your goodness all the days of my life. I will practice temperance and self-control. My speech will be kind and graceful. It will edify and encourage others that I meet. People will see you, Father God, in me and know that I represent you. I will pray the prayer of salvation with them leading them to you. I will practice the peace of God that passes all understanding by keeping my mind stayed on you Father. I shall think of those things that are pure, lovely, honest, just and of a good report. I shall believe the report of the Lord. I am your ambassador here in the earth. Use me for your glory. This is your servant's prayer. Amen.

COMMUNICATING WITH GOD

Pray without ceasing.
I Thessalonians 5:17 (KJV)

Prayer is the key to a good life because it is communication with God. The best conversation that you can have, is one with your heavenly Father. He gives us revelation knowledge, revealing things to us that we would not otherwise know. He gives us wisdom to do the right thing and be a blessing. He gives us understanding when we are perplexed about a situation or task. He gives us words of instruction to follow the right path. He will even warn us of danger ahead. He is so awesome! Pray always.

Father God, your word tells me to always pray. I will never give up communicating with you. You are my lifeline and I need your presence in my life daily. I need your continued guidance in my life. I honor and obey you. There is no one else to call upon that could do me any good. You are the great I AM. Thank you for my daily bread. Keep me from all hurt, harm, and danger. Order my steps in your word. You said if your people that are called by your name (Christians) would humble themselves and pray, seek after you, and turn from their wicked ways, you would hear their cry, forgive their sins, and cause them to have a good harvest. I thank you for the many blessings, Father. Thank you for a new day with new mercies. This is the day you have made; I will rejoice and be glad in it. Another day you have blessed me and kept me. I am forever grateful. I give you honor, glory and praise. Amen.

GIVE THANKS

In everything give thanks: for this is the will of God
in Christ Jesus concerning you.
I Thessalonians 5:18 (KJV)

Be thankful in good times as well as bad times because God has your back. No matter what the circumstance is, he will see you through it. Put your trust in the almighty God. He will lead and guide you to a safe place – spiritually and physically. Ask him for discernment of the situation so that you can recognize what is good and what is not. God is working on your behalf to make it all good. Thank him that his will is being done in your life. Allow his will to be done, not yours. Our desire may not be good.

Heavenly Father, no matter what I am going through I give thanks unto you. You are the maker and creator of all good and perfect gifts. You know about my good days and my bad days. You are with me in the valley and the mountain top. No matter what is going on in my life, you are there. So, I will thank you during the bad and the good. Your word says if I make my bed in hell, you are there. I know you will bring me through every trial and tribulation. Life can give some bad breaks at times, but you are the God of the breakthrough. You can break through every rough place and make it smooth, every valley and low place you raise it up; every mountain and hill you make it low; and every crooked place you make it straight. What a mighty God you are! You are a wonder. I trust your majestic powers. What an awesome God you are. I will praise you! Amen.

THE APPEARANCE OF EVIL

Abstain from all appearance of evil.
I Thessalonians 5:22 (KJV)

Be careful of where you are, who you are with and what you are doing. You may be innocent of any wrongdoing, but the appearance is what you have to be careful of. My former pastor was traveling out of the country for a couple of weeks. The deacons wanted to be helpful to the first lady and asked if there was anything they could do to help while the pastor was away. She told them, "No, thank you" and that everything was fine. She told me later the reason she said that. It was because she needed to avoid the appearance of evil. She didn't want rumors to start.

Heavenly Father, I realize that my physical health is in conjunction with my spiritual health. I must keep this vessel (body) physically clean as well as spiritually clean. They work together. So, I present my body as a living sacrifice, holy and acceptable unto you. Sickness and disease cannot enter this body. My body will not take part in darkness and evil tactics of the enemy. No evil shall befall me, and no pandemic shall come near me. I will stay away from that which looks suspicious. I will not be pulled into wrong crowds. Father, command your angels to protect me. I will abide under your shadow, your fortress, your safe place. Keep me near to you so that I may walk in the path of righteousness. Others may love the world and all that the world has to offer them. But for me, I will serve you heavenly Father. Thank you for satisfying me with long life. Amen.

MATERIAL POSSESSIONS

For we bought nothing into this world,
and it is certain we can carry nothing out.
I Timothy 6:7 (KJV)

Don't allow material possessions to influence you. Know where your help comes from and give God the praise each day. Sometimes people gain material wealth and forget about God. They begin to serve money instead of the one who helped them to acquire the wealth. This can lead to personal misery because when the wealth is gone, you have nothing to show for it. Don't allow greed to control your mind. Instead seek God's direction and instruction for wealth because he is the one that gives you the power to get wealth. It is not your intelligence, its God.

Father God, teach me your ways so that I will walk in wisdom. Don't let me store up material things that the moth and rust will contaminate and where thieves can break in and steal it all. Don't let me cherish or make idols of these materials belongings. You have given me the strength and ability to acquire such effects, but I will never esteem them higher than you. My heart belongs to you and not in earthly things. I will keep my mind stayed on you. I will represent you well here in the earth. I will be a conduit of blessings to your people. I will seek your kingdom and righteousness first, and everything else that I need will be added. I will not concern myself with the next day because I know who holds the next day. I put my trust in you, Father God. The love of money and material possessions will not take charge over me. You are my source and provider. You are so good to me. Thank you for everything. Amen.

THE SPIRIT OF FEAR

For God hath not given us the spirit of fear; but of power,
and of love, and of a sound mind.
II Timothy 1:7 (KJV)

We have clarity (clear thinking) because of God's power. We don't operate in fear; fear is from the devil. The enemy wants us to stay in a state of fear so he can dominate us and keep us from the life God has intended for us. God wants us to walk in his spirit-filled power, having a well-balanced life and a love for his people. He wants us to treat our neighbor as we treat ourselves.

Father God, I walk in the boldness of your love. Thank you for protection from the enemy. The enemy comes to steal my joy, kill my dreams, and destroy my future. Father God, you have come that I may have life in abundance. Thank you for giving me authority over the enemy. I take authority over every spirit of fear, every dark place, familiar spirits, wickedness in high places, wolves in sheep's clothing, bad influences, corrupt leadership, hindering spirits and any imitation of the move of God. I take authority over false witnesses, greed and gluttonous, filthiness, and haughtiness. Your word tells me that pride goes before destruction, and a haughty spirit before a fall. Father, create in me a clean heart and an upright spirit so that I may serve you in spirit and in truth. Thank you for a sound mind, a heathy mind, a good mind, a spirit-filled mind, a mind that will always stay connected to you. No weapon formed against me shall prosper. This is your servant's prayer. Amen.

SHOW THYSELF APPROVE

Study to shew thyself approved unto God, a workman that needeth not to be
ashamed, rightly dividing the word of truth.
II Timothy 2:15 (KJV)

Study diligently to understand God's word. Ask God for understanding. Ask him for wisdom. He said if you don't have wisdom, ask him for it. We study so that we can rightly divide the word of truth as we witness to others; then others will be drawn to Jesus Christ and the universal church will be added to daily. Everybody needs the Lord whether they know it or not. He is a present help in the times of trouble. We need you, Lord.

Heavenly Father, in the beginning was the word, and the word was with God, and the word was God. As I study your word, Father, I am studying your character because you are the word. When I study your character, I am studying your integrity, your strength, your uprightness, your reputation, how you interact with others, your compassion toward mankind, your ability to do good, your personality and the spirit that dwells within you. Thank you, heavenly Father for the word that directs me, corrects me, sustains me, blesses me, encourages me, gives me wisdom and understanding for the task ahead, orders my steps, and keeps me safe. Father, give me an ear to hear what thus saith the Lord, so that I may study and witness to others. Thank you, Father for my daily conversation with you. Praying your word back to you. I love you Father, in Jesus' name. Amen.

A FORM OF GODLINESS

Having a form of godliness but denying the power thereof:
from such turn away.
II Timothy 3:5 (KJV)

Beware of those who received salvation but allow it to be dormant because they love the things of the world better. These people are those who want to look the part by attending church to say that they are a member of such church. They want to relate to their co-workers and acquaintances who are religious. They feel this will have some type of influence in their sphere of friends. They are never able to come to the knowledge of the truth of the word of God. They don't study, they parade.

Father God, I declare and decree that I will always be a good witness for your kingdom. I agree with your word Father. You are Lord over my life. You have given me power over the enemy. Thank you for the gift of discerning of spirits. I will recognize that which is good and that which is bad. I come against every form of witchcraft that attempts to imitate your kingdom. I bind that secular spirit that strives to dominate the church and confuse your people. I take authority over every witch and warlock that enters the house of the God with disrespectful agendas. I bind, rebuke, and cast down every foul spirit that tends to traumatize your people. Whom the son sets free is free indeed. I declare and decree that the people of God are free from every demonic creature that is a menace to the body of Christ. As children of God, we separate ourselves from these wolves who are trying to look and act like the righteous. To God be the glory! This is your servant's prayer. Amen.

ROLE MODEL

Teach the older women to live in a way that honors God. They must not slander
others or be heavy drinkers. Instead, they should teach others what is good.
Titus 2:3 (NLT)

Be a good role model for the next generation. The older women are to be teachers of what is good and right. They are not to be gossipers but good mentors to the young ladies. They should teacher the young ladies how to be loving wives to their husbands and godly mothers to their children. When I was an advisor to the young women's auxiliary at church, I constantly told them why I was so intent on teaching them what was right and godly – it was because I did not want them to grow up being silly old women. How can we teach if we have not been taught?

Heavenly Father, I will follow your principles so that I am a good mentor for my household and my community. I will have the compassion of the Shunammite women in the Bible. I will honor your servants with a godly attitude and pleasant hospitality. I will call those things that be not as though they were. I will do this because I know your answer is "yes" and "Amen." Even if I can't see it, I know you are working on my behalf. I shall proclaim "all is well." I serve a God that is more than enough. You will supply all my needs according to your riches in glory. You own everything; therefore, my supply is always full. Thank you for your enduring commitment to my well-being. I will walk uprightly before others as I show forth your glory in the earth. Peace, joy, and happiness shall be my portion. My faith is in you, Father. I am your servant. Amen.

LIVE BY FAITH

Now the just shall live by faith: but if any man draw back,
my soul shall have no pleasure in him.
Hebrews 10:38 (KJV)

Your faith will keep you strong to go forth in the work of the Lord –
hold on! You are confirmed by your faith. You are made right and
justified by your unwavering faith in God. He delights in your commitment
to him. You rely on God because you know his word is true. Your faith in
God gives you confidence that whatever you pursue in life, God is with you.
But if you turn your back on God, he will have no pleasure in you. So, stay
strong in the word of God and the plan he has for your life. Not taking a
bow to the enemy but being loyal and trustworthy to the almighty God. Be
steadfast in your quest for righteousness.

---

*Father God, I am holding onto you. You are my provider. You supply all my needs. I
will continue to follow your teachings. My faith is built on Jesus Christ's shed blood
and righteousness. There is life in the blood and there is healing in the blood. I plead
the blood of Jesus over every area of my life and the life of my family. Jesus is Lord.
I walk by faith and not by sight. I have been redeemed from the curse. Jesus Christ
has paid the price at Calvary. I no longer operate by the world's system. My trust
and my hope are in you, Father. Thank you for your mercy and your grace. I will
not turn back. My feet are planted on solid ground. Father, you are good ground
and my faith lies in you. Amen.*

DILIGENTLY SEEK HIM

But without faith it is impossible to please him: for he that cometh to God must
believe that he is, and that he is a rewarder of them that diligently seek him.
Hebrews 11:6 (KJV)

We must exercise our faith by believing what we can't see, feel, touch, or sometimes understand. God is faithful in performing His word. So many have put their faith in other things, things that will fade away. They don't realize that the word of God is eternal and that his love is everlasting. We must diligently seek him and believe that he is who the word tells us. Noah believed God without physically seeing any evidence of what God had revealed to him. However, because of his obedience, he was an heir of God's righteousness. We must have that "now" faith, for it is what we can't see but what we believe. God honors our faith.

Heavenly Father, I believe that there is healing in your word. There is deliverance, grace, restoration, abundance, increase, and everything that I need to live a godly life. You have given us faith through your word to endure and maintain a life that is pleasing in your sight. I believe that you are a great God with great promises. I do not desire the corrupt influences of the world. I put my trust in you. I will continue to grow in your word so that you will direct me in a right manner. My faith is strong because my God is strong. Thank you, Father for your wonderful goodness. I seek to do your will. I wait patiently for you. I will not jump ahead of you. Your timing is not my timing, so I follow after you. Lead me and guide me. Amen.

DIFFERENT TEMPTATIONS

My brethren count it all joy when ye fall into divers' temptations; Knowing this, that the trying of faith worketh patience. But let patience have her perfect work, that ye may be perfect and entire, wanting nothing.
James 1:2-4 (KJV)

Don't get upset when various setbacks happen. Know that your faith is being established at a higher level so that you may be full-grown in the work of the Lord. The assessment of your faith through the setback is proof of your love and faithfulness to God. You have gained maturity, endurance, and inner peace because you trusted God through it all. Trials may come, but God is the trial lawyer. He will set you free from all persecution, giving you generously even more faith. These trials are just to build you up so that you will be developed completely in your faith.

Heavenly Father, I thank you for my good days and for my bad days. Through it all I have learned how to lean and depend on you to see me through. I know in life that hard times may come, but I am so glad that I know you in the midst of the storm. When I can't see my footprints in the sand, I know you are carrying me. I wait patiently for you to come to my rescue. You are an on-time God. You know exactly when to solve the problem and bring peace into my life. I have learned to endure the test of time. I know how it is to have plenty and how it is to have a little. In either case, my trust is in you, Father. I know that you will never leave me or forsake me. I shall not want. You are a mighty God. Amen.

DOERS OF THE WORD

But be ye doers of the word, and not hearers only, deceiving your own selves.
James 1:22 (KJV)

When we read the word, we must begin to practice the word of God. We must actively obey God's teachings. Be a practicing Christian, not a closet Christian. Otherwise, you are fooling yourself because you have not retained anything that was taught to you. A bad witness will not lead people to salvation; they will instead lead them down the wrong path. People go to church week after week and leave the same way they came in – empty. It is time to stop playing church and be the real church. Church is not a fashion show or a single's club. It is the house of God and should be respected as such. We should read the word, obey the word, and be an active doer of the word of God. Be a good witness.

Heavenly Father, my prayer is that I not only hear your word being preach, but that I will be obedient to what has been said and put my faith to the test. Your word is true. If I am a follower of you, Lord God, then I should be able to do your will here in the earth. I will keep your commandments, and I will be a good witness. I will tell the unsaved that the wages of sin is death, but the gift of God is eternal life. I will visit and pray with the sick. I will visit those in jail, clothe those who are without, tell of your goodness to those who are following after the world, and feed those who are hungry. Father, your word is hidden in my heart so that I will not sin against you. I will follow your teachings and be a doer of the word. I love you. Amen.

A SANCTIFIED HEART

But sanctify the Lord God in your hearts: and be ready
always to give an answer to every man that asketh you a reason
of the hope that is in you with meekness and fear.
I Peter 3:15 (KJV)

Honor and reverence the Lord in your heart at all times. If anyone questions your faith, be ready to give a scripture for what you believe in and do it in a respectful manner. As a child growing up in the rural section of the county, members of a different faith would come to our house to read their Bible, which was different from ours, and try to sell their reading materials to my mother. As a teenager, I didn't know a whole lot about the Bible, but I knew enough to engage them in a discussion that eventually stopped them from visiting our home. Christ is first place in my life.

Lord God, you are my everything. I honor you with my first fruits. You are Lord of my life. There is none like you in the earth. I bless your holy and righteous name. I am not ashamed of the gospel of Jesus Christ. I will study to show myself approved so that I can rightly divide the word of truth as I witness to others. I will respectfully give an answer to anyone who questions my love and honor for you. My desire is that these people will be drawn to you by what I say. There is nothing new under the sun. You are the same yesterday, today, and forever. Your word is true. Jesus, you said that you are the way, the truth, and the life. Without you, no one can come to Father God. I give you all the honor and all the glory. Amen.

CONFESS OUR SINS

If we confess our sins, he is faithful and just to forgive us our sins,
and to cleanse us from all unrighteousness.
I John 1:9 (KJV)

God gives us free will and does not make us follow Him; but if we confess our wrong doings to him, he will forgive us, cleanse us, and set us on a path of righteousness. As a child back in the day, we had something called the mourners bench at church. When you reached 12 years old, it was your time to partake in this event. We were not given the sinner's prayer, repent and be baptized; we had to get on our knees and pray for at least two hours every night until we felt God had delivered us. Prior to this annual revival session, no radio or any type of secular music was allowed. You were in consecration seeking the Lord to be saved. By the time my child was of age, the young people walked up to the pastor when he gave an alter call, and they felt an unction from the Holy Spirit that it was their time. Now, that was so much easier. God is a God of progression. Everything in its season.

Father God, thank you for cleansing me for unrighteousness. Thank you for washing my sins away. Thank you for throwing them into the sea of forgetfulness. My sins are ever before me. I have not acted according to your word. I have gone astray and allowed the enemy to trick me into wrong doings. Forgive me Father and create in me a clean heart. I have been a bad child before a good daddy. You have been so patient with me and have given me undeserved favor. I owe you so much, Father. I can never thank you enough for your saving grace. I love you and I adore you. Thank you for your faithfulness. Amen.

DO GOOD

Beloved, follow not that which is evil, but that which is good. He that doeth good is of God: but he that doeth evil hath not seen God.
III John 1:11 (KJV)

Do not follow those who are doing sinful deeds but connect with those who are doing good. For God is good, and the evil doers will be cut off. The world has so much evil to offer, it is really disheartening to the believer. If there ever was a time to pray, it is now. Pray without ceasing. Pray in the morning, during the day, and at night. We must keep our family, friends, churches, schools, communities, government, law enforcement, military, and our neighbors in constant prayer. We will imitate that which is good. We will let our spiritual light shine so that others will see our good works and they will want to be connected to our God.

Heavenly Father, I choose to follow you. Your grace and your mercy will follow me all the days of my life and I shall dwell in the house of the Lord. Your word is life to me, health to my bones, and nourishment to my body. I will not imitate the evil deeds of others, but I will follow your kind deeds. You said in your word that you wish above all things that I may prosper and be in health, even as my soul prospers. Father, I thank you that I am healthy, wealthy, and wise. Thank you that wealth and riches shall be in my household. I thank you that the wealth of the wicked is laid up for the righteous. You know the thoughts that you have for me. Thoughts of peace and not of evil; thoughts to give me a profitable and successful end. You are my Lord, my King, and my Savior. My trust and hope are in you. Amen.

ALPHA AND OMEGA

I am Alpha and Omega, the beginning and the ending, saith the Lord, which is, and which was, and which is to come, the Almighty.
Revelation 1:8 (KJV)

God is the beginning and the end. He knows all and sees all. There is nothing surprising to him. He is our all and all. He is everything we will ever need. He is the everlasting – living in and beyond all time. He has absolute control over death and the grave. He took away the sting of death. He was, he is, and he will be. He is the eternal God. You cannot get around him or replace him. He created everything – the birds in the air, fish in the sea, flowers in the field – and he created you and me. No matter what theory one can come up with, God is the center of the universe. He always has been, and he always will be. He is the everlasting Father.

Heavenly Father, you are the beginning and the end. You are so wise that you know the end from the beginning. Everything that was made was made by you. You are all seeing, all knowing, and everywhere at all times. We cannot hide from you. You hold the future in your hands. I give you, my life. There is nothing too hard for you. You are almighty, magnificent, amazing, a wonderful counselor, a doctor in the sick room, a lawyer in the courtroom, a mother for the motherless and a father for the fatherless. You are everything we need. Your mercy flows through me despite my shortcomings. You are gracious and kind. You cause long life and peace to be my portion. I am forever grateful. I love you. Amen.

WHISPER A PRAYER

Please note the following prayer was given to me while I was employed at the County School District (**Daily Prayer Coverage**). A visitor came by to see me for school district business, and before leaving, he thought to share this prayer with me on paper.

Undoubtedly, he perceived in the spirit that there was something going on with me. Actually, what he saw was my struggle with stress. He could see the stress level I was encountering at that season in my life.

The stress was so intense that my headaches were consistent, draining, and fearful. The doctors prescribed medications and different tests but there was no relief.

I said a prayer one morning. "Lord, if you think that leaving this job is what I need to do to be at peace, please have my friend call me today *(I specifically named what friend to call me)*. At exactly 4:00 pm that same day, my friend called me. I was stunned at the suddenly of God. Nevertheless, I wrote my resignation! To God be the glory! He is faithful, righteous, trustworthy, and ever present.

DAILY PRAYER COVERAGE

Heavenly Father,

I pray this prayer in the power of the Holy Spirit, the authority of the written word of God, and the victory of Jesus Christ's shed blood!!! Jesus destroyed the works of the devil and triumphed over him.

In the name of Jesus Christ, the Anointed One, and by His blood, and the word in Matthew 16:19, I bind, rebuke, and bring to no effect:

- All division, discord, and disunity.
- All rebellion, disobedience, confusion, and disorder.
- All strife, anger, and wrath, murder, hatred, and violence.
- All criticism, condemnation, and vain glory, envying, jealousy, and gossip.
- All lying hindering spirits.
- All retaliatory spirits. All deceiving and scheming spirits.
- All false teaching, false gifts, manifestations and lying signs and wonders.
- All slander evil speaking and filthy communications out of the people's mouths.
- All poverty, lack or want, and fear of lack.
- All harassing and obscene spirits.
- All fear and fear related spirits.
- All murmuring and complaining, seducing spirits, and spirits of antichrist.
- All occult and witchcraft spirits.

I break all curses that have been placed against me, and I break the power of negative words and attitudes coming out of the mouths of people. I break all generational curses and diseases. I break and render useless all prayers not inspired by the Holy Spirit, whether psychic, soul force, witchcraft, or counterfeit tongues that have been placed against me. I am free from all demonic forces, for whom the son sets free is free indeed!!! I am subject to God, and I resist the devil and he flees from me in terror!!! For no weapon formed against me shall prosper, no evil shall prosper against me, for I escape from the snare of the devil. I put on the whole armor of God. My steps are ordered of the Lord. The Holy Spirit leads me into all truth. I discern between the righteous and the wicked, between him that serves God and him that serves him not. I take authority over this day, in Jesus' name, Lord, let it be prosperous for me. Let me walk in your love and show forth your glory in the earth. I take authority over satan and all his demons and those people who are influenced by them, and I declare satan is under my feet and shall remain there. I plead the blood of Jesus over every area of my life. I am the righteousness of God in Jesus Christ, and I am saying so. I have the God kind of faith, ever increasing and limitless faith. I am God's property, so satan get out of my life, my family, my mind, my job, my body, my home, my finances, and all that concerns me!!!

I pray for the ministry that you, Lord, have called me to be part of. I call in financial support so that we can do the work unhindered by lack. I call in ministry of Helps to assist in the work. I call forth intercessors to, at all times, hold us up in prayer. I pray that all who are involved are perfectly united in our common understanding, opinions, and judgments. We stand firm in united spirit and purpose, working side by side, centering in on the Gospel of Jesus Christ. We live in harmony and unity sharing the same love. We do nothing through strife or vain glory. We follow after righteousness, godliness, faith, love, and patience, meekness, long suffering. We draw nigh to God and God draws nigh to us. I am called, anointed, and equipped to accomplish all God has for me to do. I overcome the devil by the blood of the Lamb, and the word of my testimony. I dispatch ministering spirits, angels to protect and assist me this day. I rebuke any negative expectations. I forgive all people. I receive from the Lord for He is my provider. I call forth divine appointments, open doors of opportunity and God ordained supernatural encounters, and ministry appointments and positions. I declare it is so, in Jesus' name. May the Lord perfect that which concerns me daily. Amen!!!

SALVATION PRAYER

Dear God,

I know that I am a sinner, and I ask for your forgiveness. I repent of all the bad things I've done in my lifetime. I believe Jesus Christ is your son and that he died on the cross for my sins and rose on the third day with all power in his hands.

I accept Jesus as my Lord and Savior. I will honor him for the rest of my days. Come into my life, Jesus, and give me peace, love, and joy that only you can give. Lead me and guide me, Lord Jesus, to do your will.

Thank you for saving me. I commit my life to you. In Jesus name, amen.

www.ingramcontent.com/pod-product-compliance
Lightning Source LLC
LaVergne TN
LVHW051240080426
835513LV00016B/1694